THE OTHER SHOE DROPPED

By D. L. Moutsiakis

Order this book online at www.trafford.com
or email orders@trafford.com

Most Trafford titles are also available at major online book retailers.

Printed in Victoria, BC, Canada.

ISBN: 978-1-4269-3456-8 (sc)

ISBN: 978-1-4269-3457-5 (hc)

ISBN: 978-1-4269-3458-2 (e-book)

Library of Congress Control Number: 2010907841

Our mission is to efficiently provide the world's finest, most comprehensive book publishing service, enabling every author to experience success. To find out how to publish your book, your way, and have it available worldwide, visit us online at www.trafford.com

Trafford rev. 6/7/2010

 www.trafford.com

North America & international
toll-free: 1 888 232 4444 (USA & Canada)
phone: 250 383 6864 ♦ fax: 812 355 4082

This book is dedicated first and foremost to my parents, Leonidas and Elizabeth Ann. Without their tireless effort and support, my life would have proven much shorter, and much less to my liking. This book is also dedicated to all those who have suffered from traumatic brain injury, and the people who have cared for them in their time of great need.

PROLOGUE

I

Woke up that fateful morning, looked around,
And thought: "For sure I must be dead!"
Hell was not ablaze with fire and brimstone,
But instead came in the form
Of long-term nursing care!?

Like a hibernating grizzly bear awakening from deep, dark slumber, I pried open my poor, sleepy eyes. Even before coming completely to my senses, I sensed that something here was out of whack. I willed myself awake. As I woke up, I spied my first glance at this strange, new room I found myself in. Absolutely nothing in this room looked familiar. I had never been here before…of this I was certain.

"Where am I?" I thought.

I looked around the room to see exactly what I could discover.

The room itself was rather small. The room was about one-half as large as my room in my parents' house. Two large, grey, metal doors… painted a little too hastily to suit my taste…stood on the far side of the room. Both doors were shut. On the right side of the room stood a large, solitary window whose view was partially obscured by Venetian blinds. The air was awash with the bittersweet, antiseptic aroma of a recently mopped floor. The silence in the room was deafening.

"Whoa, what's going on?" I thought. "Where am I? How did I get here?"

These seemed reasonable questions to ask myself upon awakening and not recognizing anything familiar.

"Since I was just sleeping here," I thought, "I assume that I must be in some kind of bedroom. This isn't my bedroom, though. I've never seen this room before. How did I end up in this strange room?"

This definitely was not my bedroom on the second floor of my parents' home on Long Island. The bed in my room was both cozy and comfortable. The pillow on my bed was plush yet firm. The mattress on my bed had just enough give to conform to the contours of my body, but not so much as to smother me softly with kindness. I slept most of the last twelve years of my life on that bed. I liked that bed.

This bed I was lying down on now was most uncomfortable...not at all like my bed in my parents' house. The pillow here was puny and pathetic. The mattress here was lumpy, bumpy and hard. Strange metal bars seemed to encircle me from all sides of this bed. I felt imprisoned inside some alien bed.

"Something is definitely not right here," I had decided. "I feel like I'm imprisoned in this alien bed. I'd better take a long, hard look at this room I'm in so that I can see just what else is off kilter."

I looked around this room more carefully. I was still not happy with what was staring back at me.

The room was dreary, dark and dismal. It looked like all the life had been sucked out of it. The room was clean and bare...too clean and bare to suit my taste.

"Where are all my clean and dirty clothes?" I thought. "Nothing here is out of place. Something here is definitely wrong. I have never been this clean in all my life."

The walls of my old room were painted sky blue. The barren walls of this strange room...the solitary window sill...the Venetian blinds... were all a chalky shade of antique white instead. The two doors...the guard rails of this alien bed...were a darker shade of metallic grey. There was no color in this room at all.

No vibrant, blue-and white striped curtains hung softly by the windows...as would be hanging had this been my bedroom. No bookcases...indeed, no books at all filled the room. There was just one pathetic window on the right side of the room...whose view was partially obscured by antique white Venetian blinds...that let a little light sneak in from the great world beyond.

My room had store-bought pictures on the walls, as well as blown-up enlargements of photographs I had taken of my exploits throughout Europe. There was a signed picture of the Space Shuttle Columbia that I kept from my internship at the National Aerospace Administration's sprawling campus in Cape Kennedy, FL. Where were all my pictures and my photographs? This room I was in now had none of these small details. The walls of this room were completely bare. There were just blank, antique white walls staring cruelly back at me. This **definitely** was not my room.

Or should I say the right half of my room?

Had I been fully alert and oriented to my surroundings, I would have realized right away a whole other world lay on the left side of my field of vision. I was not seeing the whole picture...not even remotely. A second metal-frame bed...with its guard rails down...stood just to my left. There were truly four walls, and not just the three walls that I had been looking at so far. Then again, had I been aware of such matters at the outset, I wouldn't have ended up in this place to begin with.

This small detail did not matter to me, though. I had already reached my own conclusion. "This is definitely not my room," I had decided. "I'm not in Lindenhurst any longer. If I'm not in Lindenhurst, then where am I?"

I pondered that question for a moment.

"Maybe I died, and am now in Hell!" I thought.

I don't remember what…if anything…triggered the next outburst… some strange word association that only I understood. All I know is that I burst out with this primal guffaw. I couldn't control myself. The thought that I could possibly have committed some cardinal sin was ludicrous. I must have spent at least five minutes in the throes of this primal, uncontrollable laughter.

"This is serious," my somber half told my more humorous half. "You just might be in Hell. Get a hold of yourself!"

I tried to calm myself down. The thought that I might actually be in Hell put a damper on my penchant for laughter. I settled down, and became serious once again. I tried to think logically:

"Could I really be in Hell? How could I be in Hell? Why would I be in Hell?" At least I wasn't laughing any longer.

"Wait a minute," I thought suddenly. "I can't be in Hell, because I'm not dead yet." I was trying to approach the situation logically…even if my logic was a little circular in nature. "I can't possibly be dead, because I don't remember dying first. Since I didn't die yet, I can't possibly be in Hell!"

There was some strange logic to this approach. Admittedly, I didn't remember dying first. I had always thought that death and dying were two things that I would remember happening to me. Since I didn't remember ever dying first, therefore I couldn't possibly be dead. Since I wasn't dead, I couldn't possibly be in Hell!

Of course, I hadn't even given the slightest thought to the myriad persons who die in their sleep each year. Did these people remember dying? I can't imagine anybody waking up, thinking to himself, "I think I'm going to die now," and then keeling over. Facts didn't matter to me much, though. I was just happy because I had concluded that I couldn't possibly be in Hell.

"Alright," I decided. "I'm not in Hell. That still doesn't answer my original question: Where am I?"

I tried to think where I could be. I had already decided that I wasn't in Hell. I looked around the room once more…hoping that something in this room would trigger some sort of epiphany. This time…sensing that I had missed something during my earlier passes of the room…I lifted my head up off the bed and forced my head to look around the entire room rather than just the right side.

On my left, I saw an unoccupied metal-frame bed with its linens neatly stacked in a pile. The guard rails in that bed were down. Between my bed and the bed to the left, a grey curtain partly obscured my view. My view of the far wall…opposite my bed…seemed strangely blurry. I thought I saw a wash basin with a soap dispenser on the far wall, with two metallic grey doors on either side. I couldn't be sure. Finally, on the right side was the aforementioned window with the partially obscured view.

I remembered seeing similar metal-frame beds with guard rails before. I tried to place where I had seen such guard rails. "Where had I seen such guard rails before?" I wondered. I knew I had seen them before, but just couldn't quite figure out where.

I pondered this latest question carefully.

"I know where I've seen such beds before," I suddenly remembered, "In a hospital! Of course, I'm in a hospital! That's where I must be."

I smiled to myself for figuring out where I was. I was in a hospital. At least I thought I was in a hospital. I was close. It was not quite a hospital. The significance of the difference between a hospital and the place I actually was would become apparent in due time.

"What am I doing in a hospital?" I wondered. "Why am I here in this hospital? What's wrong with me?"

As I pondered these questions, I took my first good look at myself. As I looked myself over, I started to realize why I was in this hospital.

I saw a pasty-skinned young man in a blue and white hospital gown lying face-up on a hospital bed. Beneath the white hospital sheets, I saw the shadow of four sticks posing as my four limbs. My pale left foot was peeking through the white hospital sheets that only partially covered my once athletically bronzed legs. My left foot was so white and chalky that I actually had to wiggle my left foot to make sure it was truly my own foot that I was seeing…not some weird, prosthetic foot pretending to be mine.

I could see that my left leg was ramrod straight at the knee, with the left foot pointing sideways out of the sheets at an angle of about ninety degrees from the rest of my body. My right leg, on the other hand, was bent at the knee so that the shadow of my right foot was flat on the bed, and my right knee stood, as if at attention, towering over my weak and miserable frame. My entire frame was covered up by white hospital sheets that were wrapped a little too tightly to suit my taste.

Fear and panic began to grip me, vice-like. Fear threatened to overtake me completely. I had to calm down. I thought back to the words from the novel <u>Dune</u> I had read that would so often comfort me whenever distressed:

"Fear is the mind killer. Fear is the little death that causes total obliteration. I will face my fear. I will allow it to pass through me and over me. And when fear has gone, I will turn the inner eye to see its path. Where fear has gone, there will be nothing. Only I shall remain."

I thought about my fear. Fear was my mind killer. I had to face my fear. I had to allow it to pass through me and over me. Only then shall I remain. Hearing these words again and again in my mind enabled me to calm myself down. I returned to the matter at hand…my pasty-skinned body.

I looked at my body lying on the bed.

"That's it!" I decided. "I've got to do something. Just lying down useless is not helping matters any. It's time for me to see if I can't get this dumb body of mine moving. Enough moping about! It's time to start moving my body around…my whole body…head to toe, starting with the head… to see what I can do."

I had already moved my head and shoulders a little when I first examined the room, as well as when I first looked myself over.

"I have to be more systematic about things," I thought. "I'm going to be a doctor in two years, for Christ's sake! It's time I started acting like one. I'm going to make this a real physical exam…starting with my head and neck. I'll move my head so that I can see how well everything works. This can be my little check-up from the neck up."

Lying face up in bed, I moved my head and neck up, down, and sideways. I lifted my head on and off the bed. I rotated my head clockwise and counterclockwise. I smiled to myself. As I smiled, I thought: "Yes, I'm smiling! Even that has to count for something!" At last I was doing something…and it felt good.

"Alright, my head and neck work. I can move my head and neck around. I even moved my head and neck to the left. Let me keep going…all the way from head to toe. How are my arms working?"

"Maybe I'd better free my arms from these damned sheets before I go any further," I thought. "Otherwise, it'll be kind of hard to test the range of motion for both my arms."

I wiggled and wormed my way under the sheets until I freed my arms from these ridiculously tight hospital sheets.

Once I freed my arms, I moved first my left arm, and then my right arm straight up and then down my sides. I rotated my forearm on each arm in turn…first prone with my thumb pointing out, and then supine with my thumb pointed toward the midline of my body. Waving both hands like Richard Nixon proclaiming that he was not a crook, I rotated my hands at the wrist. Finally, I wiggled all of my fingers.

"Yes," I thought, "My arms, hands and fingers are working just fine. So far, so good…at last I am getting somewhere."

My excitement started to build as I began moving some life back into my body. I tried to remain calm as I conducted my own, rather personal physical examination, but found it increasingly hard to do so. I felt oddly like Dr. Frankenstein…except that I was the one here alive. Despite the excitement I was feeling at moving life back into my body, I forced myself to continue my examination anyway.

My head, neck, and arms appeared to be working. I kept going with my physical exam. I tried to shrug my shoulders. They shrugged! I tried tightening and relaxing my belly…or, more correctly, the small of my back. They tightened and relaxed! I tried to wiggle my hips from side to side. Same thing!

I turned my attention once more to the sheets by my legs. I loosened the sheets round my legs by first pushing, then pulling and twisting the sheets until free. Once free, I then turned my attention to my right leg. That was the first time I realized that something was seriously wrong with my body.

The examination of my right leg began at the thigh. I tried to move my thigh in all directions. No problem. I then tried to lift my entire right leg straight up…as far as possible given the constraints of these sheets that were still a little too tight to suit my taste. The right leg lifted up. I next tried to straighten my right leg at the knee by laying my right leg flat in bed. That was a problem. My right leg refused to be straight. I was able to bend my right leg at the knee so that the heel touched my butt, but could only straighten my leg at the knee to about forty-five degrees. I tried to rotate my right foot at the ankle; it rotated just fine. I tried to wiggle my right toes; they wiggled just fine. I tried once again to straighten my right leg; it either wouldn't or couldn't lie straight.

I gave up on the right leg for now, and turned instead to my left leg…ramrod straight at the knee with the left foot pointing out to the left side. I tried to lift my left leg straight up…just like the right leg. Again, the left leg seemed to straighten just fine.

"Stay calm," I told myself. "The left leg seems to be working just fine so far. Let's keep going."

I focused my attention on the left knee. I tried to bend my left knee. The left leg refused to bend at the knee. Instead, the left leg stayed fixed at attention…apparently oblivious to the commands my mind was giving to my left leg. I tried to rotate my left foot at the ankle; it rotated just fine. I tried to wiggle my left toes; they wiggled just fine. I tried once more to bend my left knee; it either wouldn't or couldn't bend.

I couldn't believe what I had seen. Dejected by my own legs, I slumped helplessly back on the bed.

I didn't know how long I lay there on the bed like that. It could have been two minutes, or it could have been two hours. I didn't know, and I didn't care. I was in a mental fog that was very difficult to lift me out of. What finally lifted me from my fog was the realization that I was not alone.

Don't get me wrong. Nobody had come in from the outside to visit me. Nobody had come in from the outside to check up on me. What drew my attention was the fact that I was not alone. There seemed to be some sort of milky–white liquid in a plastic bag dripping slowly from one pole at the corner of my bed. I had been focused on my physical exam. I must have missed that plastic bag while looking around the room.

I stared intently at this milky-white liquid in a plastic bag dripping slowly from the foot of my bed. "What could this be?" I thought to myself. "Why is it dripping?" I willed the bag to stop dripping, but the bag wouldn't listen. I was intrigued by this mysterious milky-white liquid in the plastic bag.

I studied the plastic bag more carefully. Eventually, I would identify this plastic bag as the nasogastric feeding device used to ensure that I didn't starve to death. At the time, though, I had no idea what this could be. I had never seen a nasogastric feeding device before. The only feeding tubes I had seen in pediatrics were gastric tubes…tubes that pumped liquids directly into the stomach. I was fascinated and intrigued by this mysterious milky-white liquid in the plastic bag.

The plastic bag was connected to some kind of plastic tubing. I followed the plastic tubing. It snaked slowly down the metal pole. From the metal pole, the plastic tubing slithered and coiled across the bed. The plastic tubing seemed to fall from the left side of my bed…somewhere near my ankle…only to resurface on the left side of the bed just above my arm. The plastic tubing approached my head. Once again, the plastic tubing fell from view somewhere around my head.

I moved my hands towards my face to try to find the place where the plastic tubing had gone. I felt by my eyes. My eyes felt free and clear of any plastic tubing. The plastic tubing didn't seem to be connected to my eyes. I felt around for my nose with my fingers. I could feel something funny on the right side of my nose. I didn't know what it was.

I couldn't see or hear anything on my nose. I couldn't really smell or taste anything on my nose. Still, I could feel something on the right side of my nose. I tried to brush it off, but could not brush it off.

"What could this be on the side of my nose?" I thought. "There is definitely something on the right side of my nose."

I felt around some more to see if I could figure out what was attached to my nose. After feeling around my nose for a while, I found a loose piece of…whatever it was…attached to my nose. I did what any curious twenty-one year old person would do…I pulled on it. The piece came loose. I didn't know what it was. I didn't know where it was coming from. I just knew it came loose.

"Aha!" I thought. "The thing…it moves!" I pulled on this piece some more. The piece of…whatever it was…became even looser.

"Now we're getting somewhere," I thought. "I knew I'd get to the bottom of this. Don't quit now. I'll figure out just what this thing is on my nose. I've got hands. Pull!"

I began pulling this thing attached to my nose. The fact of the matter was that pulling on this tubing didn't really hurt. Maybe if it had hurt, I would have been more hesitant to pull it out. I didn't know if pulling on this piece of…whatever it was…was supposed to hurt or not. All I knew was that pulling on this…whatever it was…didn't really hurt.

Funny how easily this piece of…whatever it was…would come out. Putting the piece back in would prove to be not nearly as painless. That story would have to wait for the moment.

Infused with renewed sense of purpose, I grabbed this strange piece of tubing with both hands, and began pulling on it with renewed vigor until I was finally able to pull it completely free of my nose. I then held up this strange piece of tubing so that I could take a closer look at it… to see what was sitting in my nose.

What was facing me now was the far side of the plastic tubing that was connected to the bag with the milky-white liquid coming from the pole. The milky-white liquid was now dripping steadily from the plastic tubing onto my hospital gown…getting my hospital gown all wet with this milky-white liquid.

Suddenly, I felt very stupid for having pulled this plastic tubing from my nose. I didn't know what to do. Heck, I didn't even know where I was. Was I in a hospital? Who knows? I supposed that I was in some kind of hospital, but still wasn't quite sure what kind of hospital it was. To top it all off, some milky-white liquid was dripping from the bag and getting my hospital gown all wet.

I tried to actually say something, but nothing came out except for a whispered gurgle. I couldn't believe it! My mind was whirling. Some milky-white liquid was getting my hospital gown all wet, and the most I could muster was a whispered gurgle.

Suddenly, I stopped cold. I was all alone in a strange new room.

"Where are my parents?" I wondered. "What happened to them? Are they alive? Are they dead? Where did they go?" I had no idea. "Were they in a car crash?" I had absolutely no idea. My parents just were not around.

My mind was racing, pacing, and careening wildly every which way it could…trying to figure out exactly where I was and what was happening to me. The litany against fear went whirling out the window. My parents were missing. My voice was gone. I couldn't speak. My legs didn't work right. I was losing my already tenuous grip on reality.

I didn't know what to do. I tried to get out of bed, but couldn't lift myself over the metal guard rails. I reached into the bottom of my very being and let out what I thought must have been a bloodcurdling scream. Of course, it wasn't a bloodcurdling scream at all…a bloodcurdling whimper was more like it.

"Well," I thought, "if I can't let out a scream so that somebody can help me, then I'll just have to make as much noise as possible. Maybe then someone will come to this room and help me."

I didn't know what else to do.

I began by knocking down and throwing away all the sheets off my bed, and onto the floor. I next began flailing wildly whatever limbs could flail about. Down on the floor fell the plastic tubing, along with the rest of the bag with the milky-white substance. Things went flying across the room...things I never even knew I had...such as the call alarm. I was having a full-blown panic attack, and nothing was going to stop me.

I'm not sure what it was that finally caused someone to enter the room. I don't know whether somebody was just making a routine call or was responding to an alarm that I had accidentally tripped during my little flailing episode. All I know is that, eventually, somebody opened the left door of the room and entered.

Upon entering the room through the door on the left, the person saw some of the damage that I had managed to inflict upon the room. That was all it took. Upon seeing what I had done, the person quickly left.

No more than two minutes later, a veritable mob of hospital attendants, nurses and physicians burst back into my room through the door to the left of the wash basin with their needles and syringes cocked. The sight of this sea of white coats brought my little flailing episode to a rapid conclusion. The hospital attendants, nurses and physicians came at me from all sides of the bed...except, of course, the head of the hospital bed, which was against the wall. Within a minute, my lights were out, and I drifted back to a rather fitful sleep.

CHAPTER ONE

A New Year's blessing seemed to come,
With joy, and mirth, and merriment, and rhyme,
While seeming to proclaim to one and all,
How we live in such interesting times.

My name is Demetrius, and this is my story. It is a simple story. It is a story of great inspiration. It is my very personal journey from the heights of adolescent promise to the depths of rehabilitative hell, and back to a more measured and treasured existence as a Preventive Medicine physician. It is a cautionary tale. It is a tale of hope and promise.

My journey begins on the thirty-first day of December…New Year's Eve. The year 1989 and, in fact, the entire decade was coming to a close. The New Year, 1990, was rapidly approaching. The setting was a rather boisterous country pub in the quaint little village of Huntington, on the north shore of Long Island, NY.

The previous decade that finally was finishing had brought great changes to the world. Earlier that decade, Ronald Reagan, the retired movie actor and former President of the United States of America, had challenged his then political arch-rival and former Chairman of the

Communist Party of the Union of Soviet Socialist Republics, Michael Gorbachev, to tear down the Berlin Wall separating democratic West Berlin from communist East Berlin. Much to my and the world's surprise, Michael Gorbachev and the residents of East Berlin did just that. The Berlin Wall was no more. In fact, Michael Gorbachev would not rule the Union of Soviet Socialist Republics very much longer. The Union of Soviet Socialist Republics would soon be no more.

In its stead would be thirteen independent states, including the largest, a once and future Russia. Boris Yeltsin, the successor to the Communist Party Chairman, Michael Gorbachev, would rule Russia with that rare kind of chaos that could only characterize true democracy. Germany, divided since the end of the World War II over forty years ago, would once again be united…East and West Germany would be no more.

The forty-four-year long cold war between the United States and the Union of Soviet Socialist Republics at last had ended. A new decade would soon begin. A new era would soon begin. The new decade would bring great changes to the world. The new decade would bring great changes to me as well. I just didn't know it yet. Believe you me, I know it now.

That New Year's Eve, I was determined to celebrate with as much good cheer and gusto as I possibly could muster.

I had never considered myself a particularly bad-looking person. Standing somewhere between five foot ten and five foot eleven inches, I was about average height. Weighing about one-hundred-forty pounds back at that time, I was a little on the thin side. Because my arms were so long and thin back then, I sometimes imagined myself a victim of Marfan's disease, a disorder of the protein collagen associated with tall stature and long, lanky extremities. Reality was a lot simpler. I didn't have Marfan's syndrome. I was just an ordinary, black-haired, blue-eyed person with a typical Mediterranean complexion…perhaps a little on the thin side.

My most remarkable features were on my head. My deep, black hair fanned out in waves from a crest atop my head to a line just above my shoulders. My jaw protruded just a little bit at my chin. My sun-tanned nose flared out ever so slightly as it reached a point. The most remarkable features on my head by far, however, were two penetrating, somewhat inset, blue eyes that were always taking stock of my surroundings.

I remember sharing that New Year's Eve with my sister, Vaia, at that rather raucous little pub. Vaia and I used to be very close…at that time, we still were. There was a time in our lives when we could have passed for fraternal twins, even though I was actually two years younger than her. Now, of course, I was about half a foot taller than her, but there was that time when we could have passed for fraternal twins. Even after I had grown taller than her, though, we still had a bond that would take a lot to break.

I was the youngest of three children. My sister, Vaia, came before me. Vaia was two years older than me. Vaia had straight long, flowing, dirty blonde hair that stretched midway down her back. Like me, Vaia had penetrating blue eyes as well, and a generally cheerful, if somewhat oblivious, disposition. Vaia had a face that was easy to recognize, but hard to pin down. Vaia was just as comfortable in shorts and a T-shirt as she was wearing her Sunday best to church…back when she used to go to church, that is. Vaia sported a physique that was neither chunky nor malnourished, neither plump nor thin. Vaia could have passed herself off as the stereotypical 'girl next door.'

Standing at about five feet and four inches in height, and weighing about one hundred and forty lbs that New Year's Eve, she was about six inches shorter than me, even though we both weighed about the same. Don't get me wrong. No one in my family was fat…not at that time. I was the skinny one. You might say I was the baby of the family in more ways than one.

The oldest child in the family was my brother, George, who probably could have been a football player, had he ever been so inclined. Alas, George was never so inclined. George was about four years older than me. Standing at about six feet and four inches in height, and weighing about two hundred lbs that New Year's Eve, George was about six inches taller and sixty pounds heavier than I was. George had a strong, muscular frame at the time that favored his broad and surprisingly well-developed shoulders. George had dark brown eyes, deep, bushy eyebrows, a somewhat prominent jaw, and dark, black hair that had been styled on the top of his head with very tight curls.

Back then, my brother was very big into the whole black thing. He wore black shirts, black pants, black socks, and black shoes...everything he wore was black. Black was apparently very big in the late eighties and early nineties in his circle of friends, and George wasn't about to miss out on a single trend. As a result, George wore everything in black himself.

George, Vaia and I were actually three generally happy, if somewhat dysfunctional siblings...whether we realized it ourselves at the time or not. Like all calm, obedient and peaceful children, the three of us got into some rather...how shall I say...interesting physical fights. All things considered, nothing too violent took place. No one got killed, or hospitalized...nothing remotely that violent. No shattered limbs or broken bones were involved. A few minor scrapes cuts or bruises perhaps. Screaming or crying...we certainly had our fair share of both. Overall, though, I would probably characterize these fights as confounding variables in the great epidemiological game of life.

These fights were certainly interesting from an anthropological point of view, though. Often, these fights would pit George against me and Vaia. Vaia and I would gang up on George while my parents were away, and then find some way for George to get all the blame upon my parents' return. It wouldn't always be George against us, though. Sometimes it would be George and I against Vaia. Sometimes it would be George and Vaia against me. Things always were interesting in our house...never a dull moment.

George was what I might call a gentle giant. I actually did call him that...several times...although never to his face. Despite all my tricks and taunting to the contrary, I really did look up to him. I treasured our time together. During that New Year's celebration in 1990, George wasn't around with the rest of the family back in Lindenhurst. George was still working toward his doctoral degree in psychology at Wayne State University, in Detroit MI.

Vaia had graduated in 1988 with her Bachelor of Arts degree in Natural Sciences and Mathematics from Dowling College in Oakdale, NY. Vaia had taught Regents Chemistry and Earth Science at St. Demetrios, a mid-sized Greek-American parochial school in Astoria, NY.

Astoria is a section of New York City, on the northwest corner of Long Island in the borough of Queens that, at one point in time, was home to over five hundred thousand Greek-Americans...making Astoria the second largest Greek community after Athens, the Greek capital. Like most good Greek-Americans, the family lived for a while in Astoria ourselves. The three of us even went to school for a time at the very same school where my sister taught. But that was in another life.

After first teaching for a year at St. Demetrios, Vaia taught eighth grade earth science at Copiague Middle School in the village next to Lindenhurst. Vaia lived at that time with her friend and former co-worker from St. Demetrios, Amy, in Rosslyn, a relatively quiet, affluent, predominantly Jewish community on the north shore of Long Island...about half-way between Lindenhurst, on the south shore, and Astoria, on the northwest corner. Amy was a rather spirited young lady with rather definitive opinions on many subjects that she was more than willing to share with anyone who would listen. Whether at St. Demetrios of Astoria or at Amy's house in Rosslyn, Vaia and Amy spent much of that time together. Vaia would come home to my parents' home for all the major holidays, though, and Christmas and New Years Day were both considered very important holidays.

I had graduated in May of 1989 from the State University of New York at Stony Brook with my Bachelor of Arts degree in Chemistry. That fall, I returned to Stony Brook...this time as a medical student.

Stony Brook was a relatively quiet, former fishing village on the north shore of Long Island. Stony Brook lay about thirty miles northeast of Lindenhurst, on the north shore of Long Island. Long Island was basically just what you might expect…a long, thin ribbon of land…with New York City on the western side of the island, and the Hamptons and Montauk Point on the eastern side of the island. Stony Brook was situated almost halfway between New York City and the Hamptons.

New York City was actually the result of bringing together the towering skyscrapers of the island of Manhattan (which most people meant when referring to New York City), the island of Staten Island (which almost no one remembered), a sliver of the mainland known as the Bronx (which almost every 'native New Yorker' tried to forget about), and the western parts of Long Island known as Queens, in the northwest corner, and Brooklyn, in the southwest corner.

The eastern part of Long Island was split into two sections…the Hamptons and the North Fork…by the waters of the Peconic bay. The Hamptons, on the southern fork, with Montauk point at the east end, were once small fishing and whaling communities first inhabited in the early seventeenth century by hearty New Englanders. Some parts in the Hamptons have remained quaint little fishing communities, although almost nobody whales any longer. Many homes in the Hamptons, however, have been squeezed out by the overwrought mansions of the nouveau riche. The North Fork, by contrast, is a little more agrarian in nature. Large tracts of land along the island's North Fork have become the home of a hugely profitable wine industry.

Spanning the length between New York City on the west end and the Hamptons on the east end were about fifty miles of suburban sprawl on the west and about thirty miles of the closest thing to a rural section that you might expect so close to New York City on the east. This strange combination of city life, rural life, suburban sprawl, and just about everything in between was what was known as Long Island, or, as some 'native' Long Islanders would say, "Lawn Guy-Land."

The village of Stony Brook lay about halfway between New York City and the Hamptons. Stony Brook lay on the north side of the island, facing the Long Island Sound and neighboring Connecticut coastline. Stony Brook lay somewhere between the cityscape of New York City and countryside of the North Fork…never quite certain where. Most of the houses in this village were one- or two-story buildings separated from each other by small plots of trees, grass and shrubberies that, in the spring, summer and early fall provided a lush, green canopy. The two main attractions in Stony Brook village were the quaint little shops by the harbor and the State University of New York campus at Stony Brook.

The State University of New York at Stony Brook was a sprawling campus situated in the south part of Stony Brook on either side of Nichol's Road. Back when I studied chemistry and medicine at Stony Brook, the campus was in a state of perpetual construction. Bridges that led nowhere, scaffolding stretching in every direction, and buildings halfway under construction were the rule, not the exception. Now the construction has finally been completed. Back in 1990, I feared it never would be.

The State University of New York at Stony Brook campus was traditionally divided into three parts: Main or West Campus, East or Hospital Campus, and South Campus.

The Main Campus lay on the west side of Nichol's road, and included both the Arts & Sciences and Engineering Campuses. A large, flowering mall marked the middle of the Main Campus. The main campus was by far the largest, most expansive of Stony Brook's three major campuses, with the Arts & Sciences buildings on the eastern half, the Engineering buildings on the western half, and residence halls that lined the periphery.

Various buildings lined the central mall in the Main campus. The three-story brownstone Old Chemistry building situated at twelve o'clock was the site where I plodded through Physical Chemistry (or P-Chem. for short). The eight-floor ultramodern New Chemistry building...immediately behind the Old Chemistry building...was both the site where I took Organic Chemistry and the place that first launched my research career with the study of termite juvenile hormone binding proteins. At two o'clock stood the five-story Walt Whitman library where I almost never would be found, while the Administration Building that I avoided as much as possible stood at three o'clock. The Jacob Javits lecture hall, where I had all the large classes like Biology, was at five o'clock. The first two years of undergraduate training in Chemistry at Stony Brook took place at the Main Campus. My last year of undergraduate training marked my transition from Main Campus to East Campus.

Connected to the Main Campus by an underpass through Nichol's road was the East Campus. There stood Stony Brook University Hospital. Stony Brook University Hospital was considered by some the crowning achievement of the Stony Brook campus. Stony Brook University Hospital...the brainchild of what I had long considered some crazed sixties-era individual...was a many-tiered monstrosity even before they added the twin parking garages at either end of the complex. Stony Brook University Hospital stood like Plymouth Rock on the eastern side of Nichol's road; the Main Campus, the South Campus, and most of the Residence Halls lay on the western side of Nichol's road.

The entire structure was situated on a slanting hill so that the lower entrance to the basic sciences tower on the north end stood on the second floor, while the higher entrance to the main hospital on the south end stood on the fifth floor. Reaching above the ground levels of the complex were three towers, also of different heights: the nine-story basic sciences tower, the nineteen-story clinical sciences tower and the twenty-story hospital tower.

The basic sciences tower was the smallest and northernmost of the three towers; its rooms were devoted primarily to basic medical sciences such as biochemistry, pharmacology and physiology. This tower stood from the fifth floor to the ninth floor over the ground level two floors below it on the third floor. The only connections between the basic sciences tower and the rest of the world were two elevators in the center of the tower and a bridge on the eighth floor connecting the basic and clinical sciences towers.

The clinical sciences tower was the middle child, so to speak; its various rooms were devoted primarily to more clinical medical sciences such as internal medicine and surgery. This tower stood as two blocks rather than only one. The lower block stood from the eighth floor to the twelfth floor. The upper block stood from the fifteenth floor to the nineteenth floor. A bank of five elevators stood in the middle of this tower. In addition to the bridge connecting the basic and clinical sciences towers, two sets of bridges connected the clinical sciences towers to the hospital. The lower set of bridges connected the ninth, tenth, and eleventh floors to their counterparts in the hospital tower. The upper set of bridges connected the sixteenth, seventeenth and eighteenth floors in a similar manner.

The southernmost tower, the hospital tower, was the place where acutely ill patients got better. This hospital tower stood as a twin behemoth in its own right from the hospital entrance on the fifth floor to the twentieth floor with one central bank of elevators off to the side that connected the nether reaches of the first floor to twentieth floors of the hospital. From one of the central elevators, one could walk to either one of the hospital towers or to the clinical sciences tower just to the north, at the appropriate floors. That was the monstrosity known as Stony Brook University Hospital.

The South Campus lay on the west side of Nichol's road about a mile south of the Main Campus...separated from the Main Campus by a small thicket of woods and brush. The South Campus housed the School of Dentistry and the Marine Sciences Institute. I had very little contact with the South Campus. My only connections to the South Campus were through the Dental School. First and second year dental and medical students shared several courses such as anatomy, physiology, pathology or pharmacology.

I spent most the last year of undergraduate training and first two years of medical school studying at the East Campus of Stony Brook.

When not studying, I lived off campus for two years with two other roommates, an anthropology graduate student and a theater major, in a shared house owned by the Greek Orthodox Church of the Annunciation in East Setauket. I enjoyed the freedom of living off campus. Living off campus enabled me to separate my life as a medical student from the rest of my life.

Every school morning, I either drove my car or rode my bike… depending on the weather…the three or so miles from my house on Sheep Pasture road to Stony Brook University Hospital. The ride was very pleasant and quite relaxing. Sheep Pasture road was a winding two-lane road that actually had ample shoulder room for bicycles to ride…for most of its stretch, at least. Whenever the weather permitted, I would ride my bicycle beneath the dark canopy of maple and oak trees that lined the path the three or so miles to the East Campus.

Like my sister, Vaia, I, too, would come home for the major holidays. Christmas/New Year's Day/winter recess…depending on how you called them…even in medical school…were major holidays…even if not as expansive during medical school as my undergraduate days. Therefore, I was at my parents' house that holiday season as well.

My sister and I spent that particular New Year's Eve celebration together in the village of Huntington. You might ask me how I could possibly be celebrating anything involving alcohol when I was only twenty years old. Ah, the wonders of fake identification never ceased to amaze me!

Parts of Long Island could be very upscale and affluent. For example, the village of Great Neck, which was a very upscale village on the North Shore of Long Island just east of New York City, won fame as the fictitious 'Great Egg' in the novel The Great Gatsby by F. Scott Fitzgerald. Parts of Huntington, on the North Shore of Long Island east of Great Neck rivaled the Great Egg with respect to poshness and privilege. Estates near the Long Island sound were often set so far back from the main entrances as to be practically invisible. My sister and I sometimes pretended that we, too, were posh and privileged. Of course, we both knew better; we were neither posh nor privileged.

No one in my family was rich. I knew rich…such as a dental student named Joanne who was studying to become an oral surgeon. Her parents lived in a mighty fine, five-bedroom house in Huntington overlooking the water. Her father owned his own pharmacy. Her family was certainly well off.

Or, if you prefer, there was my good friend from dental school whose name really was Rich. His father, coincidentally, also owned a pharmacy. His parents had given him a Bavarian Motor Works upscale sedan and the use of a rented property at no cost for him. Seven years later, he would have a five-bedroom, four and one-half bathroom mansion on a one acre estate in the tony Long Island village of Upper Brookville with three cars in his garage…an exclusive Austin-Martin, two upscale Bavarian Motor Works (BMW) fine sedans…and the fourth car, a Jeep 4X4, that he preferred to drive around the town in. Both Rich and Joanne were rich.

Compare that to me and my family. Were my parents rich? No, they were not. My parents were both secondary school teachers. Did I drive any fancy foreign sports cars? No, I did not. I drove a 1989 compact, white Volkswagen Fox/Polo. Did my parents drive fancy cars? No, they did not. My parents drove the people's cars of Germany, Volkswagens, as well. Volkswagens suited us just fine, thank you very much!

Where did my parents live? My parents lived in a small, blue-shingled, three bedroom Cape Cod style home with one-and-one half levels on one eighth of an acre, or some similarly ridiculously small plot of land. The house sported a living room overrun by books, papers, and twelve-inch LP records, a kitchen-dining room combination stocked with enough food to feed a small army for several weeks, the three aforementioned bedrooms each styled in their own lived-in appearance, and two bathrooms of no special significance. The north shore of Long Island might have been upscale, but the south shore was definitely more working-class. My parents' home may have been small, but at least I could say it was home.

This small plot of land in the working-class neighborhood of Lindenhurst, with its three trees and its Cape Cod style house, was diligently guarded for fourteen years by my faithful attack dog, Joanie Newton Buffy, or just Buffy.

Buffy was a truly menacing animal, wasn't she, though? Adopted from the North Shore Animal Shelter, Buffy was reputed to be a St. Bernard puppy. What a lie! Instead, Buffy turned out to be this mid-sized mutt or mongrel that stood about two feet tall when on all fours… with long, wavy, mostly white hair across her head, neck, and back, accented by the occasional black splotch.

Buffy, with her white-and-black appearance, reminded me of a Holstein cow that I had seen on one of my trips to Germany. Don't get me wrong, though. I loved Buffy to pieces. Buffy was a spirited and playful dog. I just have to laugh when I think how anyone could possibly have mistaken Buffy for a St. Bernard.

Buffy lived out most of her fourteen-year-long life in the yard outside the house, leaving her domain on her leash once every day…weather permitting…to go for her little promenade with my mom through the neighborhood. During the day, from her throne…an oversized lawn chair with its blue-and white cushions…Buffy reigned supreme over any would-be denizens of our small plot of land. At night, Buffy slept in her own dog house adjacent to our living quarters.

Buffy's one big trick was barking. Could Buffy ever? Buffy would bark and bark! You name it…squirrels, rats, raccoons, opossums and other wild animals that somehow ended up on our property…and Buffy would bark at it, and chase it up one of the trees. Buffy would also bark at any person or automobile that approached her domain. I could not believe how many people were actually terrified by our 'killer Buffy.' This was patently ridiculous; Buffy wouldn't harm a soul. Menacing? Hah!

Going back to my story…

Here we were in Huntington…my sister and I…ushering in the New Year with a rather raucous crowd at one of our favorite pubs in Huntington…counting down on the television screen with Dick Clark the seconds until the New Year arrived. As the time approached, the gathered crowd roared: "10, 9, 8…" My sister and I were both caught up in the roar of the crowd.

I looked forward to the upcoming New Year with gleeful, almost giddy, anticipation. What great plans I had for that New Year! I was going to finish my two academic years at medical school and start my clinical clerkships. Soon I would be a full-fledged doctor with a practice of my own.

I kid you not! I was only twenty years old, and already in my first year of medical school. While most others my age were juniors or seniors in college, assuming that they were not already out working somewhere in the real world, I had already finished my undergraduate training, and was in my first year of medical school. What was I doing already in medical school? I was doing very well in medical school, thank you! I suppose that I had what could be described as a charmed life. I knew from a very young age that I was special.

I would also find a wife. At least I thought it was a wife. Or was it a husband? I wasn't quite sure back then. I guess I was a little confused at that time. What did you expect? I had been so focused on my studies. I finished high school by sixteen, and college by nineteen. Who could blame me for not dealing until medical school with those adolescent antics that I had somehow avoided in high school and college? Oh, well, I thought, I would just have to deal with these things later.

Of course, perhaps these musings were more than mere adolescent antics. After all, didn't my brother George tell our parents a few years back that he was a homosexual…that he was gay? That sure had brought a shock to the whole family at that time. Having a gay brother…wow… that changed everything. Who knew? Maybe I was secretly gay, too, but didn't have the nerve to tell anyone. Maybe I didn't tell anyone that I was secretly gay because all this time I had been hiding it from myself. After all, I loved my brother. Maybe that made me gay. I was what you might consider a little confused at that time.

As the New Year approached, though, none of these people…none of these issues were on my radar, though. My gay brother, my angry father, my disappointed mother…all of these people would have to wait. Counting down the seconds until that New Year, I was footloose and fancy free. I had to take advantage of life's little joys while I still could. Like all things…both good and bad…these joys, too, would soon pass.

I was drawn back to the roar of the crowd counting down the seconds to the New Year. Counting turned first to yelling and then to roaring. The countdown to the coming year reached a fever pitch: "3, 2, 1. Happy New Year!"

New Year's Day came to Huntington and the rest of New York, and there was much rejoicing. My sister and I toasted once again to the New Year at our raucous little pub in the village of Huntington. We laughed at the thought of some of the silliness and general stupidity awaiting our return home. Eventually, we drove back home to my parents' house, got ready, and went to bed. I must have slept at least one-half the day away on that New Year. I think I woke up sometime around three or four o'clock the following afternoon. Welcome to the last decade of the twentieth century.

In the light of the new, more promising year that had just arrived, I hearkened back to the events that had transpired during the previous decade. I thought about Ronald Reagan, Michael Gorbachev, Boris Yeltsin and the Cold War that was no more. I thought about the Berlin Wall and my friends and relatives in Germany, sharing their New Year's festivities for the first time in a long time as one nation under one banner. For my friends in Germany, the New Year had come six hours earlier than it did in New York. I wondered what thoughts crossed their collective minds as they toasted this last decade of the twentieth century. Here in New York, I wondered to myself what great adventures awaited me as the upcoming decade arrived. I wondered about many things at this time. I was about to find out.

CHAPTER TWO

Do you know the way to San Jose?
I'm going back someday
For piece of mind in San Jose

I was born on 14 October, 1969, in San Jose, California, and yes, I still know the way to San Jose. San Jose was the place where my mom had met, and married, my dad. Interestingly enough, neither my mom nor my dad was actually from the Bay area. My mom lived in Quapaw, OK, before moving to Los Angeles. She began training at San Jose State University with hopes of studying medicine. My dad was a Greek National...born in Greece just three years before Greece was overrun by the Fascist and Nazi regimes. After a traumatic introduction to the world, my dad decided to study archaeology in the United States.

My parents met, and married, in San Jose. They had three children while living in San Jose. I was the youngest of three. Despite having lived in San Jose for over three years of my life, I can recall absolutely nothing about San Jose. While both my brother, George, and my sister, Vaia, can recall several places and events from San Jose, I recall nothing.

While living in San Jose, my dad still yearned to return to his native Greece. Therefore, when I was three years old, my entire family packed up and left San Jose for Greece. The family lived for six months in my father's country village in northern Greece while my parents tried to launch a cheese factory.

I can recall strange and silly things from this first stay in Greece. I recall myself as a two-foot-tall munchkin running through fields of wheat that were taller than me. I also recall sneaking out with Vaia, who was five years old at that time, in the pitch dark of a moonless night…with only one flashlight to guide us…almost a mile from my grandmother's house in the middle of the village to my parents' house… past snake holes and howling wolves…because I wanted my mommy. I can also remember a family of four struck by lightning during one of the flash thunderstorms that struck the countryside late every August in northern Greece. My overall impression of my stay in Greece that year was a happy one, however, despite that unfortunate incident.

A military uprising in Greece put an end to my father's plans to stay in Greece. Don't misunderstand. My dad made very good and tasty goat cheese. He even won first prize at the International Fair in Thessaloniki, Greece, for his delectable goat cheese. Unfortunately, on account of the coup d'état that year, conditions were simply no longer economically favorable for our family in Greece.

After our first unsuccessful attempt to stay in Greece, we moved to Spain for a year. My mom found a teaching position at the American School of Madrid…a school designed primarily for the children of diplomats and businessmen. Since I turned out to be such a child prodigy, and since day care proved too expensive a proposition, my parents enrolled me in kindergarten at the tender age of three.

Like my first recollections from Greece, my recollections from Spain were sporadic at best. I remember strange words and phrases like the "Plaza de la Colon," where we stayed, and "Valencia," where I first saw a real, live orange in a tree instead of in a grocery cart. I remember our downstairs neighbor's dog named "Cheekie." The things that one remembers can be strange indeed. Spain for me overall was a good place, however. In addition to learning English, I even started to pick up some Spanish.

After the year in Spain, and a brief summer stay in my maternal grandparents' summer home in Bodfish, a quiet village in the mountains outside of Los Angeles, CA, my family moved to Astoria, in New York City.

My family lived on the third floor of a four-story apartment building off Ditmars Blvd. and 19th Street...across the street from Astoria Park. I am still amazed to see how easily I adjusted to yet another strange new environment. The three of us...George, Vaia, and I...spent almost all of our free time frolicking in the park...playing long-forgotten games like hide and seek, dodge ball, jacks, hopscotch and so on.

I first started elementary school in Astoria at a nearby public school where, according to my parents, I was quite the little gangster. At the tender young age of four, I had already developed a knack for getting others to do their dirty work for me. I befriended several bigger, older kids who offered to help me in exchange for my doing their homework. Some of the help these bigger kids did included beating the crap out of anyone who bothered me. That was about the time my parents felt it best to enroll me in elementary school at the Greek Orthodox parochial school of St. Demetrios of Astoria, where my sister would later work for a time.

I spent the second through fifth grades at St. Demetrios in Astoria. I was a diligent little student. As one of the perquisites of attending St. Demetrios, I learned to read, write, and speak in Greek in addition to English. Learning Greek would later prove very handy indeed.

I spent the next year once again with my family in Greece. I finished sixth grade back in Pinewood Schools of Thessaloniki, an English-speaking American school not too far from my father's village in the neighboring province. Greece was no longer under a military junta, but rather was a democracy once again. Thus, the odds of doing well in Greece were a little better this time than last.

Pinewood Schools of Thessaloniki was the first school that truly recognized my talent for learning. Because I was new to Pinewood, I was tested to see what level I should attend. Even though I was only entering the sixth grade, I tested as a student in the middle of the eighth grade. Therefore, I was placed in the eighth grade class. I did very well that year in Greece. During the week, my mom and dad taught, while the three of us studied our lessons. During the weekends, we stayed in my father's village in the neighboring province.

I enjoyed that year in Greece. As a sixth grader in a class of eighth graders, I learned much just by watching and listening to others. Of course, I had more than my fair share of fun that year. I enjoyed field trips to the White Tower in Thessaloniki, the ancient amphitheater in Philippi, near the eastern Greek city of Kavalla, and the caves of Petralona. I also enjoyed playing the Fool in Shakespeare's King Lear. The irony of my playing the Fool escaped neither me nor my English teacher. All in all, that year in Greece was an exciting year.

The following year, the family returned stateside once more, and finally settled on Long Island, NY...about thirty miles east of New York City...in the village of Lindenhurst, where, on account of my age, I was placed back in seventh grade. Having already completed eighth grade at Pinewood, I was simply bored out of my skull for being forced to learn seventh grade material again.

Furthermore, the initial transition from private school to public school was not a happy one. Having just moved from Greece, and before that, Astoria, I didn't have any friends that I could turn to. Junior high school on Long Island in the late twentieth century was all about being in the right clique; I wasn't in any clique. I was not a happy camper.

Therefore, when it was time for all the high school students to take their New York State Regent's examinations, I asked if I could take the New York State Regent's examination in ninth grade mathematics, also known as Algebra. After some spirited prodding from my mom, who was, after all, a math and science teacher, the school acquiesced. Not only did I pass the exam, but I got every single question correct. I did not make a single mistake. Therefore, I started the following year, the eighth grade, studying tenth grade mathematics, also known as geometry, instead of studying eighth grade mathematics once again.

By the time I reached Lindenhurst high school, I was much better adjusted to life on Long Island. I had made new friends, and had new interests both in school and out. Besides being in the Lindenhurst marching band, track & field team, and tennis team, I was a National Merit semifinalist. I enjoyed singing in the chorus, and playing the son, Patrick Dennis, in the musical *Mame*. High school was a very busy time, filled with plenty to do. I graduated from my local high school third in a class of about 450.

While still a senior in high school, I had already taken all the mathematics and chemistry courses available. Therefore, at the bright age of fifteen, I took college calculus and chemistry in the evening at the State University of New York at Farmingdale. I got all A's in both courses. At the age of sixteen, I graduated from high school and transferred to the State University of New York at Stony Brook with enough college credits to begin my undergraduate training as a college sophomore.

As a sixteen-year-old sophomore, I began studying college courses like Organic Chemistry with classmates at least three to four years my seniors. By the age of seventeen, while still a sophomore studying Chemistry at the State University of New York at Stony Brook, I received guaranteed, early admission to Stony Brook medical school so that I could free up my time for other pursuits, including basic cancer research that would ultimately result in two publications, including one as first author.

I had officially started medical school at the State University of New York at Stony Brook by the age of nineteen even though I had taken several courses in the medical school the previous year. I can report my accomplishments now with some pride. Twenty years ago, I was a little shier; I might have preferred some other, less flattering terms.

By the age of twenty, I had already carefully planned out my entire future. After I finished first the basic scientific portion and then the clinical portion of medical school, I would finish first my internship and then my residency program, perhaps in a program such as pediatrics. After all, I was always great with kids. Three more years and I would finally enter the real world as a medical doctor, fully licensed and Board Eligible in Pediatrics.

I wish I could say that my social life was as carefree and happy as my academic pursuits. Don't get me wrong. I was by no means either a monk or a hermit. I had my fair share of friends and extracurricular activities. I sometimes feel that I missed out on something because I spent so much time in academic pursuits. Perhaps these musings merely represent a secret longing to recapture the innocence of a time long since forgotten. Alas, I will never know.

It's not that I hadn't had any girlfriends while attending SUNY Stony Brook as an undergraduate. At that time, I had had two girlfriends... not at the same time, of course. Actually one girlfriend, and one... how shall I say...fling? My brother's coming out of the closet, however, made me think that perhaps I, too, was secretly gay. I was confused. Homophobia...the whole idea seems so silly now. I can remember the fights...mostly between my brother and my father, but sometimes including me, my mom, and even my sister. I can only hope that all this bickering and infighting has finally ended. One can always dream, can't one?

To this day, I still do not know whether or not my issues with my brother adversely affected my relationship with my former girlfriend. By and large, I suspect that my brother had nothing to do with my former girlfriend. As I see it, my girlfriend had her own issues that had nothing to do with either me or my brother. I had to ask myself whether any of her issues affected me or not. Basically, her issues did not affect me. It didn't matter. She wasn't my girlfriend much longer.

As the last decade of the twentieth century approached, I reflected once again on the events in my life to date. I had reached the last decade of the twentieth century. The world had much in store for me. What truly interesting times I lived in. I wished for an enchanted existence. I should have been more careful what I wished for.

CHAPTER THREE

All things, both good and bad, in the end pass
So that we can to simpler things return.
The hidden danger in not coming down, though,
Is that we might crash and burn.

As the next eighteen months of my life progressed from that most auspicious New Years' Day in 1990, the events unfolding before my eyes exceeded all my wildest dreams. Life was better than I thought possible. As I saw things, the world was now my oyster, and I was its shining pearl. The Lord, God Almighty, was smiling down upon me. I could do no wrong.

The second semester of medical school at Stony Brook went even better than the first. During the previous fall, I had resumed my cancer research at the Veterans Affairs Medical Center while still studying for medical school. In May, I presented the results from my basic cancer research before the annual meeting of the American Association for Cancer Research in San Antonio, TX. By June, I successfully completed not only the rest of the course requirements for the first year of medical school, but also the second-year course, Pharmacology…with honors in most of these courses as well! Expectations were being exceeded everywhere imaginable.

Having successfully completed all my course requirements, I celebrated that July by romping through Europe. My whirlwind tour began with a Lufthansa flight from New York City to Germany, home of my good friend and fellow medical student, Christoph.

I first met Christoph the previous summer. As a graduation present for finishing my undergraduate training magna cum laude, I went on my first trip by myself through Europe. My trip began with a flight on Icelandair from New York City to Luxembourg, where I visited a cousin and his family. I then took the train from Luxembourg to Heidelberg, Germany, where I visited with another cousin who was studying at the University. After that, I took the train from Heidelberg to Greece.

While riding the train to Greece, I met a German medical student named Christoph. Over the course of the two-day train ride, we became friends. I invited him to stay with me and my parents in Greece. He accepted. We stayed there for a few days. After that holiday, we stayed in touch as pen pals.

The following year…to reciprocate for my parents' hospitality… Christoph's parents invited me to their house in northwest Germany. We celebrated the better part of the week swapping stories, making new memories, and basically having one hell of a good time.

After relaxing and making merry for about a week, I first bid farewell to Christoph and his family, and then took the train to Greece to visit my parents in my father's village in Greece. After staying for a while with my parents, I took the train back to Germany to bid a final farewell to Christoph and his family, and then flew back to New York City.

In August, I stayed in my parents' house in Lindenhurst while my sister went to Greece. During the weekdays, I conducted additional basic cancer research at the Veterans' Administration Medical Center in Northport. Weekdays in August consisted mostly of work and study. I was always careful to combine my work in cancer research during the week with a little play time on the weekends, though. On Long Island, there were always plenty of places to discover, and I intended to discover every one before I left Long Island.

By September of 1990, I had returned to medical school at Stony Brook to study for the second year. That year, much like the first year of medical school, proved yet another busy year. In addition to studying for the second year of medical school and conducting research at the Veterans' Administration Medical Center, I also tutored first-year medical and dental students in courses such as Anatomy, Microbiology and Pathology. The second year of medical school was proving to be every bit as busy as the first year of medical school.

During the previous spring, a second-year medical student colleague named Frank had organized a student exchange between our medical institution and the First Institute Pavlov Medical School in St. Petersburg, Russia, still known at the time as Leningrad. Fourteen medical students from Stony Brook traveled to Leningrad for two weeks. In the fall of 1990, fourteen medical students and two physicians from what was then still known as Leningrad stayed for two weeks with medical students from Stony Brook, while learning how the medical system in Stony Brook differed from the system in Leningrad. I helped the Russian medical students by giving them a brief tour of New York City, Long Island, and Washington, DC.

In March of the following year, 1991, I traveled with the second contingent of second-year medical students to what was once again known as St. Petersburg as the second part of the international exchange program. In my short stay in St. Petersburg, I learned a lot, not only about the differences in medical care in the former Union of Soviet Socialist Republics, but also about the many problems we shared in common.

Besides learning about the differences and similarities in medical care between the two countries, I learned about the simple life of working, everyday Russians living behind the former Iron Curtain. I bore witness to the continuing, sad plight of innocent Ukrainian children…now staying in St. Petersburg…suffering the unfortunate effects of the catastrophe at the nuclear power plant in Chernobyl. I also witnessed the pride of a nation, or more properly, several nations, determined to rise from the ashes of the post-communist fires like an Eastern European phoenix in the rising sun. That experience served to further enrich my understanding of the ties that bound us all together.

The following month, in April, I returned to Stony Brook from my two-week stay in St. Petersburg. That month, I also submitted as first author to the journal <u>Cancer Research</u> the results of my research, which I had conducted for the last three years. I had been conducting basic scientific research on how certain proteins called metalloproteinases played important roles in the spread of cancer cells from, say, the colon, to more distant sites such as the lungs. By the summer of the following year, my findings would be published in a peer-reviewed journal. Imagine that! My first publication as first author! Was I excited? You better believe I was excited!

In May, I finished the last formal classes for my second year. I had passed all of my formal coursework. I had even completed several of the courses with honors. The next step required to advance to the clinical phase of medical school was a two day, twelve-hour examination called Step One of what was then called the National Board of Medical Examiners, but would in time become the United States Medical Licensing Exam.

Whether at one of the sunny beaches along the north shore of Long, when the weather was inviting, or at the library of Stony Brook University, when the weather was not, I studied intently for that examination. To me, doing well on this two-day examination was one way of validating all the hard work that I had done for the past two years. I had to make sure that I did well on that exam. That meant studying long and hard to make certain that I did very well.

In the early part of June of 1991, I took Step One of the National Board of Medical Examiners examination. I would not learn the results of that exam for almost eight weeks. Not surprisingly, I was a little exhausted from the many hours, days, and even weeks studying. I take that back...I was completely spent. Therefore, I took a well-earned break from the ardors of medical school to visit friends from Germany and generally vacation around Europe before resuming my medical training.

The first stop in my triumphant European tour was the town of Kleve in northwest Germany to see my good friend Christoph at his parents' house. I toasted the successful completion of the first part of my medical training with Christoph and his German buddies. Had I toasted a little too much!? What did I care? I wasn't driving anywhere.

After staying with Christoph, his family, and his friends for about a week, I took the Eurail train from Germany to Brindisi, Italy. I then hopped on a ferry from Brindisi across the Ionian Sea to the island of Corfu, or, as the Greeks say, Kerkira, in northwestern Greece. Once in Kerkira, I romped around the island...feasting, making merry, and just having a good old time. After painting the town...blue and white, of course...the national colors of Greece...I returned by ferry and train to Christoph in Germany, and then back by airplane to New York.

That June of 1991, everything in my life appeared to be going beyond belief! I didn't know what was better...traveling to Russia in March, submitting my first publication that April, passing Step One of the National Board of Medical Examiners in May, or vacationing to Europe that June. I was the international jet-setter celebrating my good fortune as best I could. I was simply having too much fun!

By the tender age of twenty-one, I had already done what others only dream of. I had traveled to eighteen countries in two continents. I had finished two years of medical school at a time when most other students my age were only preparing to enter medical school. I had presented the results of my research at the American Association of Cancer Research, and would soon publish my results in <u>Cancer Research</u> as well.

I was flying so high I could have flown from Germany to New York without an airplane. Just give me a runway, and I would have flown right home. When I left for Europe that summer, I was certain the whole world was smiling down upon me. I was no longer Demetrius, the mild-mannered medical student trudging through a dreary, drab existence. I was now Icarus the half-Greek, soaring through the summer sky.

I wish that I had paid closer attention to the unfortunate ending to the story of Icarus. According to the story, as the sun beat down on Icarus, his wax wings melted, and he went crashing down to Earth near the modern-day Greek island of Icaria. The same was about to happen to me, too, in just a slightly different way. I should have been more careful.

The first shoe dropped as I returned to John F. Kennedy international airport in New York from my whirlwind tour of Germany, Italy, and Greece, and Lord, I had to say, were my wings ever tired!

I returned from my flight to Europe jet-lagged, exhausted and entirely out of sorts. Thank God I managed to travel very light on that trip. I was lucky. All that I had were my backpack, a few changes of clothes, a well-tied mat, and some duty-free souvenirs I had picked up at the airport in Germany.

Still, tired as I was, I was somewhat surprised to see my mom minus my dad at the arrival terminal at John F. Kennedy international airport. "What could be going on here?" I thought to myself. "Where is dad?"

I began mulling in my mind possible reasons why my dad might not have been there. Was it the traffic? I was returning from Europe that Sunday. Traffic should have been pretty light. Heck, summer just started. There shouldn't have been all that much traffic. Besides, traffic alone couldn't explain things. If traffic had been an issue, then neither of my parents would have been waiting for me. Neither of my parents should have been teaching…it was summer recess…schools should have been closed for the summer. Besides, it was Sunday. There was no school on Sundays.

"Maybe my dad dropped my mom off at the terminal so that he could park the car?" I thought. I supposed that was possible.

"Oh, well, I'm sure there's some logical explanation that I'm sure I'll learn about in due course," I said to no one in particular. At that point in time, I was just too tired to care.

As I approached my mom at the arrival area, I waved to my mom. My mom waved back to me. When I approached my mom, I gave my mom a big hug and kiss. After first exchanging pleasantries, my mom turned to me, and said:

"Meme," my mom said. Meme was my parents' nickname for Demetrius. There is actually a rather funny story behind the nickname that I will share with you later. "I'm afraid that I've got some bad news. Your father can't come to meet you at the airport. He just got out of the hospital."

Whoa! Hold on, there! What was she talking about? My dad just got out of the hospital!? I didn't even know my dad was ever in the hospital! What was he doing in the hospital? This is dad we're talking about. Dads don't get sick. Is one of our friends sick? That must have been it. My dad must have been seeing somebody at the hospital. This must have been the reason dad could not come to the airport with my mom.

Up until that point, neither of my parents had ever been sick. Neither my mom nor my dad had ever been sick enough to require hospitalization as far as I could remember. I had seen sick people before, of course. After all, I worked in a medical center, and was studying to be a medical doctor. I had even been to some funerals. For some reason, though, I never associated death or disability with my parents.

"Wait a minute," I asked, "Why is dad in the hospital? Is he seeing somebody in the hospital?"

Of course, my dad was not seeing somebody at the hospital. That was not the reason that my dad did not join my mom at the airport. That was not the reason at all. As my mom walked with me from the arrival terminal to the parking garage situated across the street with my backpack in tow, my mom explained the situation to me.

"No, your father was not visiting anyone in the hospital. Your father was a patient at Syosset Hospital," my mom started. "I'll start with the short version of the story first. We can go into more depth later."

My mom continued her story as we walked toward the parking lot: "One Friday evening in early June," while I was somewhere in or over Europe, "Your father decided to stay up late to watch television. I went to bed early that evening…exhausted from another week in the blackboard jungle. The next thing I know, your father woke me up… screaming that he was going to die."

"A little while before that, your father had been lying calmly on the couch watching TV. Suddenly, he felt a sharp pain on the right side of his belly just below the ribs. He got off the couch, went into the kitchen, and drank some soda in order to soothe what he thought was just indigestion," my mom said. Drinking soda was probably one of the worst things my father could have done; drinking carbonated beverages of any kind only exacerbated the pain he had already been feeling.

"Your father was convinced that he was going to die," my mom continued. I didn't remember the exact words my mom used when describing my dad's pain, but I supposed that it didn't really matter. One thing was certain: his pain was very real.

My mom continued: "Your father started screaming at me that he was going to die. He told me to take him to Syosset [Hospital]. He was acting crazy! He was making me crazy. Therefore, I called an ambulance to take him instead. The way dad was ranting, I thought that we both just might end up in a ditch somewhere if I tried to drive him to the hospital in his condition."

Just before I had flown to Europe that June, my dad had complained of a pain in the right upper quadrant of his abdomen. Besides musculoskeletal pains, there were few causes of pain in this part of the body. Two of the more important organs were the liver and the gall bladder. I told my father that I thought it was either his liver or his gall bladder, and that he should have them checked out by our family physician, Dr. Mavrogeorgis. I then flew from New York to Europe for my holidays. I don't remember if my dad ever followed up with my family physician or not. In the end, this was just another moot point.

As my mom and I got into my mom's car, drove up to the booth, paid the parking attendant, and then drove back from the airport to our house in Lindenhurst, I let my mom tell the rest of her story.

"I waited at home for the ambulance to come. It must have been sometime around midnight Saturday morning. Finally, the ambulance arrived and took your father to the HIP Medical Center in Syosset. I then tried to go back to sleep. I did say 'tried'."

"I got up later that morning, got ready quickly...for a Saturday morning...and then drove as quickly as I legally could to HIP Medical Center in Syosset. When I arrived, I was greeted by the receptionist and a nurse. When the nurse saw who I was, she thanked me for coming so soon, and asked me if I could calm your father down for her. I told her that I would try."

"The nurse then took me to your father's room. Your father was lying in bed in obvious agony. His skin was as yellow as a summer squash lightly sautéed in butter or olive oil. It was not a pretty picture."

"I tried to calm your father down. Trust me...it wasn't easy. He screamed because he claimed all the doctors were quacks. He screamed because, he said, no one told him what was going on. He screamed because, he said, nobody was taking his pain seriously. He went on and on for at least half an hour. Finally, after your father expended the rest of his energy with his ranting, he calmed down."

By the way, HIP stands for 'Health Insurance Plan' of Greater New York. HIP referred to the type of medical insurance my parents had. No, my parents were not hippies. My parents certainly never summered in Woodstock, NY, and never took part in the Age of Aquarius. They were just ordinary work-a-day adults.

"Eventually," my mom told me, "The doctors were able to figure out what was wrong with your father. Your father had obstructive jaundice due to gall stones."

That was what was wrong with my dad. I should have guessed as much already. My dad had gallstones.

Bile is a thick, dark green liquid substance that helps in the digestion of fats and, to a lesser extent, proteins. Bile is first produced in the liver and then stored in the gall bladder, right next to the liver, until it was time to eat. For reasons that are not entirely clear, bile that is normally supposed to be secreted into the gut instead becomes stuck in the gall bladder or bile duct, causing a whole host of problems.

This is what had happened to my father. Bile had become stuck in my dad's gall bladder or bile duct, and couldn't be released into my dad's gut. As a result, the bile backed up into my dad's liver instead, and caused all kinds of problems, including jaundice, a condition in which the skin, including the whites of the eyes, turns yellow. The medical term for the condition my dad suffered from was obstructive jaundice due to an inflamed gall bladder, or cholecystitis.

In fact, my father's gall bladder, with all its bile and assorted by-products, had become very inflamed from the blockade of his bile duct. His gall bladder had become infected, and threatened to tear through the wall of the gall bladder and infect the entire peritoneal cavity. The doctors treated my dad with broad spectrum antibiotics in an attempt to calm the raging infection. Eventually, the fevers subsided.

After first being admitted to the HIP medical center in Syosset, NY, with a fever of unknown origin, my father was ultimately diagnosed with cholecystitis, prescribed antibiotics for the infections and narcotics for the pain, and released from the hospital until the more definitive cholecystectomy (operation to take out his gall bladder) could be performed as an elective outpatient procedure.

My mom was not quite finished with her story. She continued:

"After your father was admitted to the hospital, I called your brother and your sister. Your brother, George, was still in Detroit getting his Ph.D. in psychology. He flew down to New York right away. I called your sister, Vaia, too, but she wasn't at her home in Melbourne FL. It turned out that Vaia was already driving up from Florida to introduce the family to her new boyfriend, Andrew."

"Vaia hadn't learned what had happened to your father until Vaia arrived on Long Island. When Vaia and Andrew visited your father in the hospital, your father called Andrew "son"…which made Vaia very happy."

"One more thing…while your father was in the hospital…Andrew proposed to Vaia, and Vaia accepted."

That was it, then. While I was enjoying myself in Europe…visiting friends, having fun, and basically just goofing off…my dad had his first near-death experience with an almost-but-not-quite perforated gall bladder!

My mom and I talked about what had happened to my dad for most of the forty-five minute drive from John F. Kennedy international airport to my parents' house on the south shore of Long Island in the working-class village of Lindenhurst.

When I got back to my parents' house from the airport, I found my dad exactly where my mom told me he would be…lying on the couch at home in pain. The pain was no longer the 10 out of 10 when my dad first had this ordeal. Now, his pain was probably more of a 2 or 3 out of 10. Dad's great adventure with modern medicine was far from over, though. One thing was clear, though…my parents would not be vacationing in Greece that summer.

June of 1991 proved itself to be quite an interesting month for all of us after all. I took Step One of the National Board of Medical Examiners. After successfully completing Step One of the National Board of Medical Examiners, I enjoyed my last summer by myself in the hills, valleys, cities and shores of Europe.

In the meantime, while I was vacationing innocently enough across central and southern Europe, my father was recuperating at home from his first near-death experience with a perforated gall bladder. My parents' plans for vacationing in Greece that summer went whirling out the window faster than a whirling dervish in the Turkish sun. As I pondered my fate, I wondered what new surprises July and August had in store.

I was about to find out.

CHAPTER FOUR

Summertime back here at home,
Although the living was not easy,
Maybe something here was jumping,
But it was not fish or cotton...

July of 1991 came at last. I started my third year of medical school at Stony Brook. The third year marked a significant shift in learning. Instead of simply studying the basic scientific aspects of the medical field in the classrooms or lecture halls, I would now be learning the clinical aspects of the medicine from the bedside. As I was about to discover, there was quite a lot about medicine I had to learn. There was much I would learn the long, grueling and difficult way.

The third year of medical school began...rather like the first year... with a daylong series of orientation sessions at Stony Brook University Hospital. For the first time in quite some time, I was able to forget about the ongoing problems with my dad in the hospital long enough to actually learn something.

During these orientation sessions, the one-hundred-twenty-or so third-year medical students were reunited once again...after having spent the last two months either studying for Step One or recovering after having taken Step One of the National Board of Medical Examiners. It was refreshing to see so many familiar faces…fresh, energetic young faces eager to tackle the latest obstacles standing in their collective paths. It was also refreshing for me to start some real work; it would take my mind off my father and his gallbladder.

There was much to do on this day. First, all of the incoming third-year medical students had to attend lectures marking the various milestones we had to pass in order to advance to the fourth and final year of medical school. Next, we were introduced to the appropriate etiquette and demeanor expected of us as ambassadors of our profession. After these lectures, we then dispersed so that we could complete the various necessary tasks such as obtaining the proper identification badge, or receiving the requisite short-length lab coats that marked our status as third-year medical clerks.

By five o'clock, orientation day at Stony Brook University Hospital had ended. I was excited. I would soon see my first real patients at my first hospital…Nassau County Medical Center in East Meadow, about twenty minutes west of my parents' house by car…depending, of course, upon the traffic conditions. Infused with renewed sense of purpose, I drove the roughly fifty-five minutes from Stony Brook back to my parents' house in Lindenhurst.

The previous month…just before flying to Europe…I had moved my stuff from East Setauket back to my parents' house in Lindenhurst. I knew that I would be spending much of my time near my parents' house in Lindenhurst while studying at various local hospitals such as Southside Hospital or Nassau County Medical Center. Therefore, I had decided to move back with my parents in order to save rent expenses and the like.

The next day couldn't come soon enough. The next day marked my first day as a third-year medical clerk at Nassau County Medical Center. Nassau County Medical Center was another sprawling medical campus about twenty minutes northwest of Lindenhurst…ten minutes northeast of HIP Medical Center in Syosset…and five minutes due west of Mid-Island Hospital in Bethpage. The importance of each location would soon be apparent. I spent that night eagerly anticipating what new adventures awaited me at Nassau County Medical Center.

For the first day of my medical clerkship, I intended to be the best-dressed third-year medical clerk possible. I wore medium brown dress slacks, a light-blue, long-sleeved, button-down shirt with a patterned brown tie depicting a scene from the Far Side comic strip, matching blue socks and brown shoes, and a shiny, full-length white lab coat for my new position at Nassau County Medical Center.

The first day of work at Nassau County Medical Center began in much the same manner as my first day as a third-year medical student at University Hospital at Stony Brook…with yet another orientation session. Apparently many of the same issues that needed to be addressed at Stony Brook…such as parking permits and additional identification cards…also needed to be addressed at Nassau County Medical Center before I could actually see patients. The first day of work at Nassau County Medical Center consisted of enough orienting to last me into the next millennium, or so I thought anyway.

The following day, after having finally addressing all of the issues that needed addressing, and orienting myself to all the places that needed orienting, I began life as a third-year medical clerk at Nassau County Medical Center.

My first clerkship at Nassau County Medical Center was pediatrics. Pediatrics was the study of diseases among children. Pediatrics was yet another word derived from Greek. Am I ever glad that I studied Greek at St. Demetrios while living in Astoria! 'Pediatrics' comes from two words: 'Pedia,' which in Greek means children, and 'Iatric,' which in Greek means doctor.

Pediatrics proved to be a very exciting clerkship. I liked studying pediatrics. At the time, I could easily have seen myself becoming a pediatrician. Who knows? Perhaps I would have felt the same way about all my clerkships had I been able to experience all of them in the same manner as pediatrics. Alas, I will never know; that was simply not to be. All I could say about my clerkships was that I learned a lot during my short stay in pediatrics.

While a third-year medical clerk in pediatrics, I had my first chance to learn some standard medical techniques…like drawing venous blood or obtaining arterial blood gas from children. Drawing blood from children was rarely if ever something that was easy to do; in fact, it almost never was. For many children, the mere sight of a needle within sticking distance of a nurse or medical student was enough to send that child into a titter from which that child could not be easily calmed. I knew right away that obtaining blood samples from screaming children would not be an easy affair.

Still, obtaining blood samples…even from screaming children… was something often very necessary to provide a proper diagnosis or to monitor progress. If I wanted to be a good pediatrician, I felt that I had to be able not only to obtain blood samples, but to do so as painlessly as possible. Therefore, I learned various inventive new techniques to obtain blood samples.

One technique involved drawing venous blood as quickly as possible to minimize trauma. Another technique involved actually talking to the children and parents before sticking a child to explain to them what I had to do and why. I appeared to have somewhat of a knack for calming crazy children down with a combination of good humor and a cheery disposition. Who knows? Maybe I would have been a good pediatrician after all given the right opportunity.

Life in the pediatric ward, of course, was about much more than simply designing creative new ways to torture unsuspecting children with the tools of phlebotomy. I also learned about medical problems that children got themselves into, whether due to genetics, accident or design, and some of the cures and treatments medicine had to offer.

Some medical problems, like incurable cancers, reminded me of the limitations of modern medicine. I saw a four-year-old boy and their parents coping as best they could with glioblastoma multiforme, a rare and highly lethal form of brain cancer. On the other hand, I also saw an adolescent with Hodgkin's disease, a cancer of the lymph nodes that, with appropriate therapy, is often now curable

Seeing that adolescent cured of her Hodgkin's disease was a truly uplifting site that reminded me why I entered the field of medicine in the first place. I also saw a child with rheumatic fever…a consequence of a recent, untreated strep throat. This child reminded me what could happen if early infections go untreated. Seeing children in the clinic for their well child visit was also uplifting. I got to see healthy, active children doing what healthy, active children did best…acting like children.

All of these clerkship experiences were what I considered real-life learning experiences for me, the patient, and the patient's family and friends. I liked these experiences. I liked pediatrics. I liked working with kids. I really liked working with kids. I thought that I just might become an excellent pediatrician.

This first clerkship of my medical school career was going about as well as could be expected…considering that my father was at home recovering from his first near-fatal incident with an inflamed gall bladder. I was learning from my patients and from my books about diseases such as rheumatic fever and celiac disease. I was learning about parents and children and some of the ties that bind them tightly together. I was enjoying learning. I was enjoying the opportunity to help the little ones and their parents deal with some of the hardships of life.

Of course, I often wonder if I would have felt the same about all the other clerkships. I had not yet experienced internal medicine, surgery, family medicine, obstetrics & gynecology, or psychiatry…pediatrics was my first clerkship. Would I have felt the same? Those points would soon all become moot.

Just when it seemed that I might actually start enjoying my third-year medical school experience, the first shoe struck back again. <u>The Revenge of the Gall Bladder</u>, that strange new melodrama starring my father as the patient, returned with a vengeance. None of the events in my life would have transpired as they did, had my father's simple, elective cholecystectomy actually been what it was supposed to be...a simple cholecystectomy. Thank God for small favors!?

While I was studying pediatrics at Nassau County Medical Center, my father had been recuperating at home in Lindenhurst from his first great adventure with his gall bladder. While not entirely back to normal, he had regained much of his stamina. He would soon need all of the strength he could muster to stay alive.

At the end of July, after having recovered enough from his first bout with his gall bladder, my mom took my father back to the HIP Medical Center in Syosset, for what was supposed to be an easy elective cholecystectomy. He would have his simple surgical operation, wait a few hours in the recovery room, and then return with my mom to the house to recuperate. That was the plan, at least. Easy, right!? Easy was hardly a word that I or anybody else in the family would use to describe it.

On a typical summer day on Long Island...somewhat hazy and humid...toward the end of July, while I was learning pediatrics at Nassau County Medical Center, about twenty minutes northwest from my parents' house by car, my mom drove my father back to the HIP Medical Center in Syosset, for what was supposed to be a simple, elective cholecystectomy. From the outset, however, the procedure proved to be anything but simple.

First, the surgery was delayed by about four hours on account of a gunshot wound that required the more immediate attention of the surgeon, Dr. Grauer. Next, once the surgery commenced, the surgery took over twice as long as originally anticipated. Instead of lasting just over two hours, as originally anticipated, the procedure lasted almost five hours. While I was learning real-life pediatrics, my father was under the knife, and my mom was worried sick.

When the surgeons finally did close my father up almost nine hours after the surgery was scheduled to begin, the surgeons left behind little pockets of bacteria that soon multiplied, and became bacterial abscesses festering in his belly. Because the surgery had ended so late, the surgeons had decided to keep my father overnight for observation. That was the first thing they did that appeared to be correct. The following day, my father began to spike fevers that kept him in the HIP Medical Center in Syosset until the cause of the fever could be found and eliminated.

That was simply not the way things were supposed to be this summer! My mom and dad were supposed to be vacationing in their country villa in the northern mainland of Greece. My parents had already purchased their round-trip tickets to Greece. By now, my parents should have been in faraway Greece enjoying the sun, sand, scrumptious desserts and finest dining this land had to offer. Instead, my father was hospitalized in the HIP Medical Center at Syosset…with recurring fevers…while my mom was shuttling back and forth between Lindenhurst and Syosset… tending to my dad as often as allowed. There would be no vacation in Greece for my parents that summer.

The end of July of 1991 proved to be as interesting as the previous month, but for somewhat different reasons. My dad was once again hospitalized with complications from what was supposed to be simple elective surgery. My mom was taking care of my dad as best as she could during what was supposed to be her summer vacation in the Greek countryside that simply never materialized.

Where was I while my parents' house of cards came crashing down? I was everywhere and nowhere at the same time. I was in too many places at once. On the one hand, I was a third-year medical student studying pediatrics during the day at NCMC in East Meadow, NY. On the other hand, I was a son visiting my father at the HIP Medical Center in Syosset, NY, as often as possible. In addition, I was a third-year medical student studying for my upcoming pediatrics examination whenever I got the chance. Let us not forget I was also a human being, who only occasionally remembered to eat and sleep. I was wearing so many hats, that I feared they would just fly away with the first stiff breeze…leaving me confused and befuddled. I was at wits' end. I wondered how long this could possibly last.

Life was too stressful for me and my parents that July. My parents and I were all stressed out, and dreading the ill effects this stress might ultimately bring.

Now, I mentioned earlier that there were two other children in our family…in addition to me. Where were my brother and my sister while our world was crashing down around us? Why wasn't either one of them able to help us during what was so obviously the summer of our discontent?

My brother, George, had been in Detroit working on his Ph.D. in psychology during the last two years. George was still in Detroit working on his Ph.D. in psychology. I believe that George was in his final year of his doctoral studies. George had many things to do that year, such as finish his doctoral thesis, and defend his doctoral thesis in front of committee members. As a result, George wasn't around to help us.

My sister, Vaia, was no longer teaching eighth grade Earth Science at Copiague Middle School. After graduating from college in Oakdale, Vaia had earned her provisional license to teach Biology and General Science in the secondary school in New York State. However, Vaia's provisional license was about to expire. In order to get her permanent certification, Vaia had to get her Master's degree in education or a related field. Therefore, Vaia had moved the previous year to Melbourne, FL, to earn her Master's degree in education. Vaia was still studying toward her Master's degree. As a result, Vaia wasn't around on Long Island either.

Thus, out of the five of us in the family, only the three of us… my mom, my dad, and I…were around on Long Island. My dad was hospitalized at the HIP Medical Center in Syosset, NY. My mom was doing her best not to get too stressed out while tending to my dad as best she could. I was doing my best not to get too stressed out while shuttling between Nassau County Medical Center for my medical training, HIP Medical Center in Syosset for my father, and Lindenhurst for my fleeting rest. My dad was doing his best just to stay alive.

That was July of 1991 for me and my parents on Long Island. The summer of 1991 wasn't looking very good up to that point. The summer of 1991 was about to get much, much worse for us.

August started in about the same manner as July ended. The daily grind remained much the same in early August as it was in late July. For me, the daily grind entailed waking up every weekday at some ungodly hour, getting ready for my clerkship, battling the early morning traffic in the car to Nassau County Medical Center in East Meadow, NY, and studying nine or ten hours a day in the pediatric ward. The daily grind also entailed driving back home in the evening traffic, eating dinner, studying some more for my upcoming exam in pediatrics, and finally sleeping.

The weekends were reserved for doing all my neglected chores such as paying my bills. The weekend was a time for studying for my upcoming pediatrics exam. The weekend was also a time for visiting my dad in the hospital.

My mom's daily grind included waking up, getting dressed, and going to visit my father at least once a day at HIP Medical Center in Syosset. My mom's daily grind also included taking care of the necessities such as paying the bills, doing the laundry, mowing the lawn, caring for our dog, Buffy, and going grocery shopping. My mom's daily grind also included occasionally remembering to eat and sleep.

My dad's daily grind involved just staying alive...a feat that he would have to do were he to see me through what I was about to befall.

Our daily grinds continued for the next two weeks. After finishing the final two weeks of this agonizing encounter, my clerkship in pediatrics was about to come to an end. The last day of work for my pediatric clerkship was Wednesday, 13 August, 1991. The final examination in Pediatrics was scheduled for that Friday, 15 August 1991.

Wednesday, 13 August 1991 was also the day the other shoe dropped.

CHAPTER FIVE

For diff'rent people,
Diff'rent things stay etched within their minds.
For some, it could have been a birthday
Or perhaps a wedding day.
For me, it was the thirteenth day of August
That remained forever etched
Within my mind.

The place was the bicycle path between my parents' house in Lindenhurst and Bethpage State Park, on the eastern edge of Nassau County, on Long Island. The date was Wednesday, August 13, 1991. The time of day was the late afternoon or early evening. This was a place and date that would forever remain etched within my mind. That was the day I had my bicycle accident.

For reasons that I still cannot completely understand, I can recall some of the most intricate details surrounding both the bicycle accident itself and the first twenty-four hours after that freak accident that would forever change my life. That was my bicycle accident. The other shoe had dropped.

Even now, I would hardly have imagined all the hysteria surrounding this seemingly insignificant event in my life had I myself not lived through it. I sometimes wonder myself what the big deal was all about. Wow...I had a bicycle accident. Big deal!

Perhaps you had ridden a bicycle when you were young. Perhaps you still ride a bicycle recreationally later in life. Perhaps you can even remember falling off the bicycle, and scraping your knee or bruising your elbow. You may wonder what the big deal was about having a bicycle accident.

To me and the unfortunate few who have had similar experiences, that tiny little bicycle accident was anything but tiny. That bicycle accident was a big deal. That bicycle accident was a very big deal indeed!

To this day, almost twenty years after the bicycle accident, I can still remember some of the most intricate details surrounding the accident... such as my silver and black Nike-brand sneakers with the bright green stripe or my black bicycle shorts with the neon green stripe. At the same time, I can recall next to nothing about the two months I spent in a coma following my accident. While I can remember so many intricate details about the bicycle accident and the first twenty-four hours after the bicycle accident, I can remember basically nothing about the following two months.

I suppose that I shouldn't have been too surprised by this selective amnesia that I experienced. People really do experience selective amnesia. Selective amnesia does not just take place in situation comedies or soap operas. Where had I first heard of selective amnesia in medical school? I remember...during neurology class in my second year of medical student.

I remember learning in neurology class about several neurological conditions. I learned about cardiovascular conditions affecting the brain...such as stroke. I learned about primary brain cancers such as glioblastoma multiforme and systemic brain cancers such as metastatic melanoma. I learned about infections of the central nervous system such as meningitis, inflammation of the lining of the brain and spinal cord, and encephalitis, inflammation of the brain itself. I also learned about a condition called epidural hematoma.

The phrase epidural hematoma comes from the Greek. A hematoma is literally a cut of blood. If that blood escapes the body, it is called a bleed. If the blood stays somewhere inside the body, it is called a hematoma, or bruise. The term epidural referred to the virtual space between the dura, or outer lining of the brain on the inside, and the bony skull on the outside. Normally, the epidural space is just that…a virtual space. Normally, nothing is found between the dura and the skull but for a few arteries, such as the middle meningeal artery, which course just inside the skull and supplies oxygen and nutrients to part of the brain.

An epidural hematoma, then, was a bruise between the skull and the dura. An epidural hematoma forms when one of the arteries lining the inside of the skull and carrying oxygen and nutrients to the brain bursts, letting the high-pressure, oxygen-rich blood gush forth into what was normally just a potential space between the skull and the brain. My neurology instructor taught me that epidural hematomas were bad things. I believed my neurology instructor then. I believe my neurology instructor even more now.

My neurology instructor continued…

When one of these arteries burst, blood would come gushing from the confines of the blood vessel that had previously contained the blood. Unfortunately, once the blood was free, there was no place for the blood to go. The bony skull made certain of that. Not having anyplace else to go, the newly free, high-pressure arterial blood would push against the neurons of that person's brain, and ended up actually shoving the person's brain matter against the other side of the skull.

If left untreated, just about everyone who has an epidural hematoma dies of the hematoma. I think my neurology professor reported one unverified account of a person with an epidural hematoma who survived without treatment…my memory is a little fuzzy here. Even with the appropriate surgical treatment…which involved drilling holes into a person's skull to relieve the tension from the high-pressure, arterial bleed…as many as two in five, or forty percent, of patients with epidural hematomas died. There was no non-surgical treatment for epidural hematoma. Without surgical intervention, just about everyone dies. Perhaps in the future this will change, but until that time, surgery remains the only viable option.

The image of an epidural hematoma conjured up by this neurology instructor was both strikingly vivid and at least a little gruesome. Still, that wasn't what proved to be the most interesting feature. What had always been the most interesting feature to me, in a morbid sort of way, was the following:

Although many people who suffered epidural hematomas would lose consciousness at first, just about every person who initially lost consciousness would regain it, and actually feel fine for a time. For some, that time might have been twelve hours; for others, that time could be as long as five days. These persons would walk, talk, sleep, and even hold entire conversations without any problem.

Just because these persons felt fine, though, one should not assume that they were actually fine. These persons, blissfully ignorant of their impending doom, would go about their daily routine, while high-pressure, arterial blood was filling up the tiny, potential epidural spaces between the skull and the outer lining of their brains.

The moment of truth would come. Eventually, the blood from the high-pressure, arterial bleed would squeeze the rest of the brain matter against the other side of the skull. All kind of nasty little things…like seizures or comas perhaps…would happen. More often than not, the person would then end up the latest specimen on the autopsy table for pathologists to pore over post-mortem.

As I listened to my neurology instructor, I was overcome by morbid curiosity. Part of me was horrified to hear what happened to these poor patients. Part of me was curious to learn what it was like to be totally lucid and yet not know what was about to happen to these patients. While the whole thing with the bleeding, compression of the brain to the other side of the skull, seizure, coma and, of course, death was most mortifying, that part about feeling fine for some time always had me scared the most. I would soon learn firsthand what it meant to have an epidural hematoma.

And now back to my story...

The day was Wednesday, August 13, 1991...just another typically hazy, hot, and humid late-summer's day. The place was Lindenhurst, on the south shore of Long Island in the western tip of Suffolk County. I had been living once again with my parents for almost two months now. I had just finished the last scheduled day of work for my pediatrics clerkship at Nassau County Medical Center in southeastern Nassau County, about twenty minutes from my parents' house by car. I had returned home early that day from yet another mentally grueling day at the hospital.

I had a lot to do. I had to study for my final exam in pediatrics. After all, the exam was that Friday at Stony Brook. I had been trying to study for the final exam as much as I could. Between long hours working at Nassau County Medical Center, visiting my father in Syosset, eating, and sleeping, I was trying to find time to study pediatrics. Studying pediatrics was proving anything but easy.

I probably should have visited my dad in the hospital like a good son. Even to this day, my dad never misses an opportunity to remind me what I should have been doing. Over two weeks had passed since my dad had been re-admitted to HIP medical center in Syosset after what was supposed to be a simple, elective cholecystectomy. Two weeks after that simple surgery, and my father was still an inpatient...too sick to be sent home. I visited my father in the hospital as often as I could. That evening, unfortunately, I just couldn't do it.

The pediatrics clerkship, the final exam, my hospitalized dad…all these factors were stressing me out mightily. The weight of the world was bearing down on my shoulders. I couldn't take things any longer. I needed to relax…to calm down…to take a break. I decided the best thing I could do was to go for a bicycle ride in order to clear my mind. On that thirteenth day of August, I went for a bicycle ride. I went for the last bicycle of my life.

You wouldn't have known just from looking at me what was about to happen. You wouldn't know this at all. After all, here I was, this goofy-looking, somewhat lanky, good-spirited young lad all of twenty-one years of age. My head was covered with this wavy, thick, black mop of hair that stopped just short of my shoulders. Deep, penetrating blue eyes beamed just below the dark brows. My winning smile was sure to save me from any hazardous situation. What could possibly go wrong with me?

My frame was lean and mean. In high school…in college…even in medical school…I had always been thin. While in high school, I ran on the cross-country team. I ran in the Long Island half-marathon during my senior year of high school…one hot day in May…and finished the race in a time of one hour and forty minutes. That same, thin physique from my high school days would carry over through college and even medical school.

Cycling came somewhat later in life than running. Sure, I used to ride a bike when I was little, but that was different. As a kid riding my bicycle, it was always about the destination. I rode my bicycle to the local grocery store to pick up a half gallon of milk. I rode my bicycle to a friend's house to play tennis or Risk™, a board game where the object was total military domination of the world. As a child, riding a bicycle was all about the destination.

Cycling was different. Cycling was about more than just riding a bicycle somewhere. Cycling was about working out…exercising the legs while clearing both body and soul. Cycling, like running or swimming, involved aerobic exercise. Like runners…especially long-distance runners…cyclists experienced what could be described as a "cyclist's high." Cycling wasn't simply about the destination…but also the journey itself. I wasn't riding my bike just to be somewhere. I was riding my bike for the sake of riding my bicycle and enjoying the ride.

Cycling didn't start out for me this way, of course. I had originally bought my new bike in medical school as a way to save gas and the environment by riding my bicycle to Stony Brook. Riding my bicycle to Stony Brook from my shared house in East Setauket took only five more minutes than driving my car. In addition, parking my bicycle by the medical school entrance was a lot easier than driving my car to the parking lot, scouring the parking lot for a vacant parking place, and then walking from the parking lot the roughly five hundred meters to the medical school entrance. What could I say? I was being environmentally conscious long before it was fashionable or trendy. Besides, I liked cycling a lot. Cycling wasn't just about a destination; cycling was fun.

During my second year of medical school, I rode my bicycle just about everywhere I could. I rode my bike from my shared house on Sheep Pasture Road to the University at Stony Brook. I rode my bike up and down the hills and valleys of Stony Brook, Setauket, and the neighboring villages of Old Field and Port Jefferson. I rode my bike from the medical school to the beach in the neighboring hamlet of Old Field to watch the sunset on the Long Island sound. I suppose the fairer question to ask was where I didn't ride my bike.

When I moved back to my parents' house in Lindenhurst that July to start my pediatrics clerkship, I brought my bike with me back to Lindenhurst. After all, it was a rather expensive bike that cost me the same as four medical school textbooks. (For comparison, each medical school textbook cost me about as much as a dress shirt, fashionable tie, pair of slacks, underwear, pair of socks and pair of shoes combined. I'm not talking thrift store either. I'm talking Macy's or J. C. Penney department store.) Whenever I needed to de-stress while in medical school, I figured I could just get on my bike and go for a bicycle ride.

That August day, after coming home early from yet another mentally grueling day at the hospital, I needed to de-stress. I **really** needed to de-stress. The pediatrics exam was to take place in just two days, and I felt woefully unprepared for it. My dad lay dying in Syosset hospital. I couldn't take it any longer. I needed to get away, and so I went for a bicycle ride. I went for my last bicycle ride of my life.

I got ready for the long bike ride in my usual way. I put on my black bicycle shorts with the bright, neon-green stripe. I could already start to see a small slice of my daily stress melt away like butter on a warming pan. I donned the black and red bicycle shirt. I put on my white gym socks with the neon-green stripes, and laced up my silver and black sneakers with the bright green stripes. Next, I strapped my black, nylon fanny pack onto my waist, tucked my wallet safely inside the black, nylon fanny pack, and then zippered shut the black, nylon fanny pack. Finally, I carefully put the Bell™ Quest helmet on my head, and snapped the helmet in place.

I always wore my helmet. Since my first fall, I decided that I would always wear my helmet.

Last year, I flipped off my bike when some car decided to make a sudden right hand turn in front of me without the courtesy of either a signal or a brake light. I flipped off my bicycle, and landed in the gravel alongside the road. I scraped my knees and arms pretty bad. From that point on, I made a point of always wearing my helmet.

After snapping my helmet in place, I went downstairs from my bedroom to the kitchen, grabbed my water bottle from the rack of clean dishes, turned on the tap for a while to let the water get nice and cool, and then filled my water bottle with water. I grabbed my water bottle, left my house through the kitchen door in the back of the house, and walked over the short stretch of recently trimmed lawn grass to the shed at the side of the house next to Buffy's doghouse. I then went into the shed, and brought my bicycle from its designated spot. Finally, I tucked the water bottle in its place on the side of my bike, climbed onto my bike, released the little parking lever on the left side of the bicycle, and was on my way.

I left the driveway of my parents' house to go for my bicycle ride. I left my parents' house to go for the last bicycle ride of my life.

The route I was to take that evening was fairly straightforward. I had taken that route countless times before. I could have recited that bicycle route in my sleep, but for the fact that, of course, I never talk in my sleep.

I would start by riding my bicycle about half a block north from my parents' house to the railroad station and then turn west at the street light onto the bicycle lane of Hoffmann Avenue, parallel with the train tracks of the Long Island Railroad. This portion of the Long Island Railroad was an elevated railroad track that ran roughly from west–southwest to east-northeast. Just below the elevated railroad on the south side, next to the bicycle path, was Hoffmann Avenue, which continued west, parallel to the train tracks. Hoffmann Avenue continued west…crossing from Suffolk County to Nassau County, until it merged with Sunrise Highway.

After crossing into Nassau County and merging with Sunrise Highway, I would keep going west on a bicycle lane next to Sunrise Highway until I reached a second bicycle path that turned north toward Tackapausha Lake, in the village of Massapequa. Once I reached Tackapausha Lake, I would leave the noise and smog of Sunrise Highway in favor of the chirping birds and occasional jogger in the park along the second, infinitely more pleasant, bicycle path.

I would continue north along this second bicycle path surrounded by trees and bushes and underbrush, first alongside the Bethpage State Parkway in North Massapequa, and finally to Bethpage State Park in Bethpage. I would rest for a bit, look around, and maybe grab a drink of water before heading on back home. By that time, my mom would be home from visiting my dad at the HIP Medical Center, and my mom and I would have a quick bite to eat at a nearby diner. That was the plan.

The trip from Lindenhurst to Bethpage went exactly as anticipated... not a single hitch. I left the house on my bicycle around 6 PM that evening, with my water bottle fit snugly in the water bottle holster of my bicycle. I rode my bicycle from my parents' house in Lindenhurst past Railroad Avenue, past Sunrise Highway, past Tackapausha Lake, and past Bethpage State parkway to Bethpage State Park.

The entire trip from my parents' house to Bethpage State Park was about fifteen miles (twenty five kilometers). The trip there took just under an hour...including stops for streetlights to turn green, stops to let parents with their little ones go by, and the like. After riding my bicycle for an hour in Long Island's midsummer haze, heat, and humidity, I was sweating salty buckets, but hey...I was working out! Wasn't that what I was supposed to be doing?

From atop my bicycle, I looked around to get a better view of my surroundings. I spied some birds chirping in the dense, green canopy interspersed amidst the open fields of the golf course. Further off in the distance, I could see two male golfers decked out in typical golfing attire...bright, multi-colored plaid pants, white shoes and solid, short-sleeved Polo shirt...who looked to be finishing up their final round for the day.

While still standing on my bicycle...with my legs balanced on either side of the bicycle...I reached down for the water bottle, grabbed the water bottle from its holster, opened the water bottle, and had a drink of water. After having been on my bicycle for an hour or so, the water wasn't very cold any more. Still, it was water, and so I gulped it down greedily.

I closed the water bottle, and put it back in its holster in the middle of the bicycle. I looked around one final time while giving myself a little rest. A female jogger...with headphones designed to block out the outside world...was jogging further along the trail off in the distance.

The two golfers, who now appeared to have finished their final round for the day, were heading back to their cars to drive to their respective homes.

I looked at my watch strapped to my left wrist. It was a few minutes after seven in the evening. It was getting late. It was going to get dark soon, and I didn't relish the idea of riding my bike in the dark. Besides that, my mom would be returning from her visit with my dad at the HIP medical center in Syosset. I had to hurry home so that my mom and I could grab some dinner before studying for my upcoming pediatric examination. Therefore, I hurriedly climbed back onto my bicycle, and high-tailed it back home.

The sun hadn't quite set just yet as I headed home. The maple and the oak trees lining the parkway, however, had become just a shade darker as the sun approached the horizon. A gentle ocean breeze had finally started to cool off the otherwise hot and humid day that was so typical of Long Island in the summer. The sun was slowly sinking beneath the sky. Soon the sun would set, and the sky would become dark. Therefore, I raced a little faster.

Robert Moses, New York State politician extraordinaire, could be considered by many the brainchild behind the beautiful park system that we now have on Long Island. Like most modern-day politicians, Robert Moses was not without his share of political controversies. If I could say just one good thing about Robert Moses, though, I would say that he designed a truly lovely park system...especially on Long Island.

It didn't really matter which State Park you were referring to... whether it was Bethpage State Park along the Nassau-Suffolk County border, Jones Beach State Park on one of the barrier beaches in Nassau County on Long Island's south shore...or even Robert Moses State Park in Suffolk County on the western tip of Fire Island, yet another barrier beach on Long Island's south shore...these were all truly good state parks. Whether at the golf courses and bicycle trails of Bethpage State Park or the sand, dunes and beaches of Jones Beach or Robert

Moses State Park, there was always plenty to be thankful for…such as the birds, the trees, and the peace of mind that one found there.

The parkway system on Long Island on the other hand…yet another concoction of Robert Moses, and by no means his best or brightest…was a horse of an entirely different color. Just the name itself…parkway… says something less than complimentary. The parkway system consisted of a series of limited access highways…the Southern State Parkway and Sagtikos Parkway, just to name a few…designed to provide those wealthy enough to afford their own automobiles access to the many state parks. The parkways were deliberately built with low-lying bridges that would allow only cars, but not trucks or buses, to pass…as a way to keep the underclass of New York City from taking over the parks.

The parkway system left one with some interesting issues regarding nomenclature. In New York, one drove on the parkway and parked on the driveway…unless, of course, it was rush hour (which on a typical weekday evening on Long Island stretched from about 4:00 PM to about 7:30 PM). During rush hour, everything was a giant parking lot, and nobody seemed to move at all.

Unlike other parkways such as the Southern State or Sagtikos Parkways, though, Bethpage State Parkway was different. Yes, Bethpage State Parkway still had a rush hour, but this was really a rush hour… not rush hours.

One reason for this discrepancy was the fact that, unlike other parkways that had two or three lanes of traffic in each direction, Bethpage State Parkway had just one lane of traffic each way separated by a double yellow line. Should just one driver chose to drive at the speed limit of 55 miles per hour, or, God forbid, even slower, every driver after him in line would be forced to drive at the speed limit or slower. As a result, most speeding drivers avoided this parkway like the plague.

Riding back from Bethpage State Park on the bicycle path alongside the Bethpage State Parkway, I glanced at the road. Traffic on this road was fairly light. I figured I could relax a little bit along the trail.

That was a major mistake.

I was riding my bicycle path next to Bethpage State Parkway... approaching the last exit on the parkway before the bicycle path veered off toward Tackapausha Park in Massapequa...when it happened...the other shoe dropped.

I was riding my bicycle down a very slight downgrade, on the right and proper side of the bicycle path...approaching an underpass just before the last exit on the Bethpage State Parkway...when I saw another cyclist riding on the wrong side of the path, coming straight at me. I saw the other cyclist rapidly approaching me. I tried to swerve to the right side of the bicycle path some more to give him room. It didn't matter.

The other cyclist hit me head on.

The other cyclist fell off his bicycle to my left, and landed on the grass. He was basically fine. I, on the other hand, flipped forward, did a somersault over my handlebars and landed head first on the broken pavement of the bicycle trail. I was not fine.

I still can't believe it! I had been wearing my bicycle helmet, strapped properly around my neck. The other cyclist was not wearing his bicycle helmet...if indeed he even had one. The other cyclist was fine. I was not. Did I think that what was to happen to me was fair? Hell, no! What's fairness got to do with this? Fairness was simply not a part of this equation.

It did not matter. There I was...splattered on the broken pavement of the bicycle path. My arms and legs were splayed in all directions...a tangled mess of cuts, scrapes and bruises. My contorted body lay in a crumpled heap. The worst, though, was the throbbing pain I felt on the left side of my head where my head, protected supposedly by the primitive helmet, made contact with the broken pavement.

I had landed on the left side of my head. The point of

was a region just above my left temple…a part of my head that was supposed to have been protected by my helmet. There would be no protection for me that day.

I managed to sit up from my sprawled-out position on the rocky pavement. My arms lay by my sides, cradling my knees, while my feet stood firmly on the ground. I took off my helmet…still intact as best as I can recall…and left my helmet on the floor by my side.

I had a splitting headache emanating from a point just above my left temple. That headache had my full attention. One thing was certain. My head really hurt. I don't believe I lost consciousness at that time. I am pretty sure I was awake for the entire accident and its initial aftermath. The collision had taken all of about ten seconds, but would change my life forever.

The other bicyclist's name was John. I don't remember why I still know that name almost twenty years after the fact. I don't remember much else about him. John appeared to be a young man in his mid-to-late-twenties. John had dark, brown hair that ended just above his shoulders and a clean-shaven appearance to his face. John had a lean, yet athletic physique. I think John might have been a real estate broker or a mortgage banker…or even a lawyer or law student. I'm not sure why I remember any of that. I just do.

John got back on his feet after having landed on the soft, green grass. As he got up, he noticed that I wasn't getting up. He left his bicycle in the grass, and hurried over to see if I was alright.

"Are you OK?" John asked me.

I don't remember what I said. I muttered something incoherent, I suppose. Can you truly blame me for muttering some gibberish? I had bigger things to worry about…like the splitting headache emanating from just above my left temple. I suppose that I was not being the most cooperative patient. What could you expect? I was in pain!

John reached into his fanny pack and pulled out his wallet. From his wallet, he pulled out a business card of some sort.

"My name is John," he said. "This is my business card."

I accepted his card. He said some more things, but I don't remember what they were. More water under the bridge, I suppose.

Some more cyclists had seen me sitting up on the pavement in the middle of the bicycle path, and stopped to examine the situation. I was barely aware of any of them. One person spoke to me:

"Should I call for an ambulance?" the person asked.

"Yes," I replied.

I don't remember anything at all regarding whom he was, what he looked like…I mean nothing other than that fact that he was male. He might have been Black. He might have been White. He might have been thin. He might have been fat. I didn't know.

Instinctively I had told the person that I needed an ambulance to take me to the hospital. I didn't think long and hard about the situation. I didn't ponder all the possibilities. My headache had my complete attention. I barely noticed my surroundings or anyone around me. I hadn't even taken a good look at myself. Had I done so, I would have known right away that I needed medical attention. Still, as a medical student, I knew enough to seek medical attention in situations such as these.

The man, who approached me earlier, approached me again and said: "I just called for an ambulance. They should be here shortly."

"Thank you," I replied.

An ambulance arrived in what could have been either two minutes or twenty minutes…I had no idea. Any concept of time that I had went flying out the window faster than my bicycle helmet, which I had long since unstrapped from my head. I didn't think to check my watch that still sat firmly on my left wrist. Had I done so, I would have realized that my watch had already gone to meet its maker.

One thing was true, however. By the time the ambulance arrived at the scene, my headache by and large had gone away, and now I just felt drained. The paramedic and his assistant got out of the ambulance. The paramedic first said something incomprehensible to the bystanders at the scene. The paramedic then turned to face me.

"Are you OK?" the paramedic asked.

"I suppose," I replied.

"What happened?" the paramedic.

I then told the paramedic briefly about my accident:

"I was riding my bike southbound on this bike trail. John approached me from the south. We collided. I landed on this rocky pavement. I had a splitting headache before, but the headache has since gone away."

After a brief assessment, the paramedic decided that my situation warranted further medical attention. The paramedic decided to take me to the nearest hospital…Mid Island Hospital, in the center of Long Island, about five minutes away from the site of the accident.

If you have never been involved in any injuries or other emergency situations up to now, don't worry. You haven't missed much. The situation, from the paramedic's point of view, was quite simple.

First, the paramedic assessed the situation: Bicyclist down on the ground.

Was the bicyclist conscious? The bicyclist was talking to the paramedic; therefore, yes, the bicyclist was conscious.

Was the bicyclist alert? Well, the bicyclist was talking with me, and having a fairly normal conversation. Therefore, the bicyclist was alert.

Next, was the bicyclist oriented to person, time and place? Well, the bicyclist said his name, Demetrius. The bicyclist correctly identified the date as Wednesday, 13 August 1991. The bicyclist said the place… on the bicycle path along Bethpage State Parkway somewhere between Bethpage and Massapequa, in Nassau County. Therefore, the bicyclist appeared to be oriented to person, place and time.

Having determined that the bicyclist was oriented to person, place and time, the paramedic tried to determine if the bicyclist needed additional medical assistance.

Did the bicyclist need medical attention? The bicyclist seemed to think so. He had just been in an accident, and thought he needed medical attention. The paramedic agreed with the bicyclist's assessment.

Therefore, the paramedic decided to take me to the nearest Emergency Room…in this case, Mid-Island Hospital.

The paramedic and his assistant laid me down on a gurney…which was basically a glorified ironing board…and strapped me in tightly. Then, the paramedic and his assistant heaved me…gurney and all… head first onto the ambulance, strapped me and my gurney in, closed the rear ambulance door, got back into the front of the ambulance, and took off on the Bethpage State Parkway northbound toward the hospital, with their sirens wailing.

It was apparently not a very long ride. About five minutes later, I arrived at the emergency room of some hospital. I knew it was the emergency room because, through the window of the ambulance in the rear doors, I could make out the words "EMERGENCY ROOM" written in bold, red lettering.

Once I arrived in the emergency room, the paramedic and his

assistant got out of the front of the ambulance and disappeared out of sight…leaving me strapped in, alone, in the ambulance. Eventually, both returned to the back of the ambulance, and opened the double doors. The paramedic climbed into the back of the ambulance, where I was still strapped in motionless atop the glorified ironing board. The paramedic then disconnected some strange device designed to keep the gurney from cruising recklessly around the interior of the ambulance whenever the ambulance moved.

Next, the paramedic in the ambulance, together with his assistant on the ground lifted me and my gurney up, and hoisted me onto something that I could not see, but could only assume must have been some sort of transport device. The paramedic and his assistant never were very big on conversation, apparently, and I was not about to distract the paramedic or his assistant with a dizzying array of idiotic questions designed solely to satisfy some strange and morbid curiosity. I thought it best to just shut up and let the paramedic and his assistant do their jobs.

After the paramedic and his assistant hoisted me onto this transport device, they first secured the gurney atop the transport device, and then wheeled me on this transport device roughly fifteen feet from the ambulance into the emergency room of the hospital. As I lay on the gurney atop this transport device, all I could think about was how long it would take them to turn off the stupid siren! The sound was killing me! When were they going to turn the siren off!?

Eventually…I don't remember exactly when…somebody did turn the siren off. As I was wheeled from the ambulance into the emergency room, I took my first look at what would become my home for the next two months. Welcome to Mid Island Hospital.

CHAPTER SIX

He tried to leave both web and loom
But stayed still strapped within the room
He knew not what tests lay in store
On coming to the hospital…

There I was…strapped into a gurney in front of the Emergency Room entrance to Mid-Island Hospital, in Bethpage, Long Island, about twelve miles northwest of my parents' house in Lindenhurst. I was probably no more than about ten or fifteen minutes south of the HIP Medical Center in Syosset, where my father had been hospitalized for more than two weeks in abject misery. Mid-Island Hospital, in Bethpage, NY, in the middle of Long Island, was a truly special experience for me. Mid-Island Hospital was the first place where I would truly enjoy all the blessings the medical system had to offer me…from a patient's perspective, this time.

I don't mean to imply that I had never been sick or never visited emergency rooms before. I had been to emergency rooms a few times in the past. Once, during a practice session of the Lindenhurst High School Track & Field club, I had tripped and fallen while running, and twisted my ankle as a result. That orthopedic adventure earned me a trip to the Emergency Room at Good Samaritan Hospital in nearby West Islip. Thankfully, after a brief physical examination that included X-ray examination of the legs, the Emergency Room physicians determined I hadn't broken anything, and eventually sent me home with an ACE bandage to wear for the next few days, and a prescription for ibuprofen (Advil), which I never filled.

Another time, not too long ago, I had scraped my knees, arms, and shoulders pretty bad after swerving to avoid a speeding automobile that had decided at the last minute to make a right turn in front of me. As I tried to stop suddenly to avoid a head-on collision with the car that was now right in front of me, my bicycle lost traction and began skidding out of control. I flipped over my bicycle and landed in the gravel alongside the road…shielded only by my outstretched arms. Once again, though, I didn't have to be admitted to the hospital from the emergency room.

Finally, a long time ago, while my family and I lived in Astoria, Queens, around the late nineteen-seventies, my mom brought me to the emergency room because I had a high fever of around 104 °F (40 °C). I believe this may actually have been my first experience with the swine flu. It does not really matter. The fever responded rather quickly to the ABCs of pediatric care…Antibiotics, Bed rest, and tender loving Care from a loved one. Yet again, I escaped admission to the hospital.

Up to now, I had been the luckiest one in my family. I had never been hospitalized. My father was currently being hospitalized for a bacterial liver infection that refused to go away. My mom was hospitalized three times…once for each child. My sister had been admitted to the hospital in Astoria, Queens…a long time ago…with a case of appendicitis. My brother had been kept in the hospital an extra day when he was born, I believe, in order to repair bilateral inguinal hernias in his groin.

Out of the five of us in our nuclear family, I had been the only one that, up until that point, had never been hospitalized overnight… except, of course, at birth. I had been working for two months in a hospital as a medical student, but that wasn't the same. I had never been admitted to a hospital as a patient before. This was the first time I had been admitted to a hospital as a patient. It would not be my last.

Upon entering the lobby of the emergency, some woman who identified herself as a receptionist approached me and my gurney atop this transport device in the lobby of the emergency room.

"Do you have your medical insurance card?" the receptionist asked.

I could immediately sense a shift in priorities from the paramedics to the hospital workers. The first thing that the paramedics had asked was whether I was alright. The first thing that the hospital receptionist asked me for was my medical insurance card.

"What would you like?" I asked as politely as possible. I was trying not to seem too snide. "You want my medical insurance card?"

I could already feel my temperature rise. With as much politeness as I could muster while still strapped within a gurney lying atop the transport device, I kindly informed the receptionist: "I can't comply with your request for a medical insurance card."

"My medical insurance card," I continued, "is inside my wallet, which, in turn is tucked carefully inside my fanny pack which is strapped around my waist which is, finally, strapped inside the gurney atop this transport device. Therefore, no, I can't provide you with my medical insurance card."

While I was speaking to the receptionist, a woman who appeared to be an emergency room physician...decked out in green hospital scrubs and carrying her stethoscope around her neck...approached me, and asked me if I could stand up for her.

My pot was beginning to boil. My anger grew like Mount Vesuvius preparing to explode. For a moment, I forgot where I was and what I was doing there.

"Are you asking me if I can stand up?" I began. In my mind, I could see the smoke billowing from both ears.

I continued: "Here I am…strapped onto a gurney atop some transport device in the lobby of the emergency room…and you ask me if I can stand up?" I was fuming now. Plumes of ash and smoke were billowing forth from my crater. "If you truly want to see if I can stand up, you can start by releasing me from these ridiculous contraptions!"

The emergency physician was temporarily taken aback.

Upon seeing the degree to which the gurney and transport device beneath it were confining me, and upon realizing that I could probably walk without too much difficulty, the Emergency Room physician motioned for the paramedic or hospital attendant to release me from the ridiculous contraptions that were confining me.

After the paramedic or hospital attendant released me from the confines of the gurney and transport device, the emergency room physician found that I was indeed able to stand up.

In as calming a voice as possible, the emergency room physician said: "Can you go behind that curtain over there," as the emergency room physician motioned to a nearby cubicle, "In order to change out of your street clothes and into a hospital gown so that I can examine you more carefully?"

"Yes," I said…having remembered once again where I was, and what I was doing there. "I can do that."

Before I changed out of my street clothes, though, I first turned to the receptionist, reached into my black, nylon fanny pack that was attached to my waist, unzipped the fanny pack on my waist, and pulled out my wallet. I reached into my wallet, and dug out the medical insurance card.

"Here," I told the receptionist, "my insurance card."

I then gave the receptionist my medical insurance card. Actually, it was not my own medical insurance card. It was my mom's medical insurance card from her position as middle school math and science teacher in New York City. My mom had been teaching for the last twelve years for the City of New York. Under my mom's health insurance policy from the City Of New York Board of Education, I was covered until my twenty-second birthday. That wouldn't take place for another two months, on 14 October, 1991. Luckily for me, I was still covered under my mom's health insurance plan. I was lucky. I was very lucky.

I then tucked my wallet back in my fanny pack and zipped it shut.

Somebody...I don't remember who...it could have been the Emergency Room physician...directed me to a little dressing area behind a curtain in the emergency room, and handed me from the pile of gowns a hospital gown that I was to wear, along with the hospital booties that I was to wear in place of my socks and sneakers. I went to the dressing area behind the curtain, closed the curtains behind me, and slowly began to undress.

First, I removed the black, nylon fanny pack that was fastened on the left side of my waist, and let the fanny pack fall gently to the floor. Next, I gently lifted my black and red biking shirt over my head. Thankfully, I suppose, I still couldn't see what had happened to my face. This dressing cubicle did not, apparently, come equipped with a mirror.

Next, I carefully took off my black bicycle shorts with the bright, neon-green stripe...stained with a mixture of sweat, dirt, tiny and not-so-tiny pebbles, miscellaneous muck and blood stains...and let my shorts fall around my ankles. After I let the biking shorts fall to my ankles, I sat down on the grey, metallic folding chair, untied my silver and black sneakers with the bright green stripes, and took my sneakers, white gym socks with the neon-green stripes and biking shorts off of my feet. Then, I put the hospital booties on my feet.

I was slow and deliberate as I was taking off the clothes because I had lots of tiny and not-so-tiny bits of rocks, miscellaneous muck, blood stains, and dirt that I was trying somewhat unsuccessfully to avoid. I put on the blue-and-white patterned hospital gown with the ties at both the neck and waist, fastened the ties together into little bows, and then stepped back out into the viewing public.

Sometime while I was changing into my hospital gown, my mom arrived at the hospital. My mom was a bit frazzled. Could you blame her? My mom had just gotten back earlier that afternoon from visiting my dad at the HIP Medical Center in Syosset, and pressed the answering machine…only to learn from some hospital receptionist's recording that her son, Demetrius, had just been involved in a bicycle accident, and was currently in the Emergency Room of Mid-Island Hospital in Bethpage…about fifteen minutes away from my parents' house in Lindenhurst. My mom rushed back in the car as fast as she could, and rushed over to yet another hospital…this time to see me.

As soon as I came out of the changing area, decked out in my blue-and-white patterned hospital gown, I saw my mom. I could sense right away that my mom was upset, and just a little bit frazzled. I was no dummy; mom was frazzled. Could I blame her? No way, no how… mom was very upset.

"What happened?" my mom demanded!

"I was in a bicycle accident." I told my mom.

"How did you…I mean, what…oh, never mind!"

Now I was really in for it. I always knew that, when my mom started to become incoherent, the best thing I could do was just to shut up and take whatever punishment was coming to me. This, I was sure, was to be no exception.

"That's just great!" my mom continued. "I just get back from the hospital to see your father when I get this message on the answering machine from some receptionist at Mid-Island Hospital in Bethpage saying that you'd been in an accident, and so I rushed over here to see what it was. Well, tell me," my mom continued in a tone of voice that was by now more resigned than upset, "What happened?"

I tried to gather my composure a little before actually speaking to my mom. Calm and poise in these sorts of situations only seemed to help.

"Well," I explained, "This is what happened. I was riding my bicycle back from Bethpage State Park. I was riding on the bicycle path next to Bethpage Parkway...on the right side of the bicycle path...when another bicyclist appeared out from under the overpass. The other bicyclist was going in the opposite direction on the wrong side of the path... straight towards me. I tried to move over to the right some more so that I could avoid the other bicyclist, but the bicyclist hit me anyway. After the two of us collided, I flipped over my bike and landed head first on the pavement. The other guy landed in the grass, and appeared fine. Somebody called an ambulance. The ambulance came, and here I am."

I thought that I had best start with the minimalist approach to the accident, and then slowly work my way up.

"That's just great!" she replied. Of course, that was not really great. My mom was actually displaying one of her coping mechanisms...in this case, a little sarcasm...in this situation. Sarcasm was one of her biggest coping mechanisms, although by no means her only one.

"That's wonderful! As if I didn't already have enough to worry about!" she continued. "How are you now? Are you all right? Does anything look or feel broken? Do you have a headache? How does your head feel?"

Asking me twenty questions…that was another one of her coping mechanisms. Sometimes my mom would hurl a barrage of questions at me just to see if I would still be standing after all was said and done. I knew I had to tread very carefully. I tried to answer all her questions as best I could.

"I just feel very tired now, and I still have a bit of a headache left over from the bicycle accident." I told my mom. "When I first fell off my bicycle, I had a really bad headache…not a migraine or anything like that…just a very bad headache. The headache seems to be going away now, though. It doesn't seem to be nearly as bad anymore."

"I also scraped up my legs pretty bad." I continued. "I got some cuts and bruises on my legs, and I got some more cuts and scrapes on my arms. It also hurts a little when I try to straighten and bend my legs around a lot." I tried to show my mom what I meant by first sitting down on a nearby chair, and then trying to alternately straighten and bend each leg in sequence. "Also, both my legs feel pretty stiff…my left leg a little more so than my right leg. I haven't even seen what happened to my bicycle. I don't even know where it is. I don't know if the paramedic took my bicycle, or just left my bicycle on the bicycle path."

My mom looked at me as I gave my little narrative. As I was talking, her whole facial expression appeared to change right in front of my eyes. It appeared to soften up quite a bit from just a few minutes ago. My mom wasn't upset with me any longer. My mom now seemed almost sorry for me. Seeing this change in my mom's facial expression, I suddenly felt very scared.

"Mom," I asked, almost dreading what she might say. "What's wrong?"

"Forget about the bicycle for now," my mom told me. "Have you taken a good look at your face?"

"What?" I asked.

The question took me aback. Actually, I hadn't seen my face. From the time I fell from my bicycle along the bicycle path by the Bethpage State Parkway, through the time spent strapped into the gurney in the ambulance, up to the time spent in the Emergency Room getting undressed, I hadn't seen my face at all.

"Maybe you should take a look at yourself in the mirror." My mom began pointing out some of the highlights of my new, unimproved appearance. "You have this big bruise around your left eye that's so swollen that your left eye is practically closed shut. The whole left side of your face is all puffed out! See if somebody at the front desk can give you a mirror, so that you can see for yourself what I am talking about."

That was news to me! In all this time that had taken place since the accident, I had never seen myself in a mirror. I had not felt my face. Suddenly, I wanted to know. "How did I look?" I wondered. I really wanted to see a mirror. Where could I find a mirror? I walked over to the receptionist.

"Excuse me. Could I have mirror so that I can get a good look at myself?" I asked.

I thought I sensed a little fear…or was it pity…in the receptionist's timbre.

"Sure," the receptionist replied. The receptionist reached into one of the drawers beneath the front desk, and handed me a small, hand-held mirror. Finally, I could see myself in the mirror.

I looked in the mirror. I did not like what I saw.

The top of my head was a tangle of hair and dirt recklessly thrown here and there. I could see the start of a big, fat bruise on the entire left side of my forehead, eye socket, and left cheek. The bruise was two very lovely shades of black and blue. My left eye was practically closed shut from the sheer size of the bruising above and below my left eye. I looked away with my one good eye. I had seen enough, and didn't want to see any more.

"We'll talk about this later," my mom said.

About that time, one of the hospital staff approached the two of us, turned to my mom, and spoke to her:

"I am going to take your son to the lab and to the radiology suite to run some tests and take some X-rays," the staff member informed my mother.

I was standing right next to my mom…right in front of this person. This person simply refused to address me…preferring instead to speak only with my mom. It was as if I wasn't there at all.

"Excuse me," I said.

I didn't know if this person was this impertinent with everyone, or was saving this treatment just for me.

"Just let it go," my mom warned me in a low tone of voice.

Normally, I would have made some pithy remark to this man for suffering his impertinence as long as I had. By this point in time, though, I was too tired to say anything pithy. Therefore, I let this person take me away for some testing and X-rays without any of my usual, snide commentaries.

My mom waited for me in the waiting room just inside the Emergency Room lobby while this person led me away somewhere I no longer remember in order to run a series of tests and take some X-rays. My mom may have stopped in the cafeteria or the coffee shop to grab a bite to eat. I don't know.

I wish that I could remember all of the tests that I had taken; as I mentioned earlier, I was simply too tired at that time to think to ask what tests I was taking.

I assume that the emergency room physician had ordered some routine blood tests such as a complete blood count (CBC) with differential to help rule out any acute or chronic, long-term blood disorders such as anemia or a high white blood cell count, which are often seen in acute bacterial infections and leukemia. Although it was probably too early in the course of my injury for me to have an elevated white blood cell count, the blood test could still serve as a baseline from which to compare future values.

I also assume that routine blood chemistry tests, and tests of the clotting system, such as the prothrombin (PT) and partial thromboplastin (PTT) times, were performed. These blood tests could give me an indication of how well my blood would clot in response to certain outside triggers.

I am pretty sure that the emergency room physician ordered me to radiology to take some X-rays of my legs. The X-rays of the legs were designed to rule out any broken bones in the legs, as well as, perhaps, certain parts, like the knees, that may have moved out of their normal alignment. I know that I took some X-rays; I just don't remember what the X-rays were for.

While in the radiology suite, I also underwent a Computed Axial Tomography (CAT) scan of my head. What did the CAT scan reveal? I honestly don't know! They never told me...neither in the beginning when I first had the scan, nor several years later when I asked for all of my medical records as part of my civil investigation of my rehabilitation. Did the CAT scan I had give any indication of the impending doom that was about to befall me? I may never know.

One thing that I am certain the Emergency Room physician did not order was a Magnetic Resonance Image (MRI). Across all of Long Island back in 1991, there were maybe two MRI machines in use; neither was at Mid Island Hospital in Bethpage.

Sometime that evening, while I was either in the lab being pricked, poked and tested, or in the radiology suite being irradiated…all in the name of modern medical science…one of the doctors involved in my case spoke with my mom. Apparently, the medical staff thought it best to admit me to the hospital overnight for observation. Because of the nature of my injury and the uncertainty surrounding its prognosis, the doctors wanted to keep me for observation so that, should anything grave or serious develop, I would already be in the hospital. Any issues would be addressed immediately.

When I returned to the waiting room after completing the battery of testing and irradiation, my mom was in the lobby waiting for me like a centurion guarding a treasure hoard. As I approached my mom, I could sense that she had something on her mind, and so I pre-empted her.

"Hey, mom, what's up?" I asked as lightheartedly as possible… considering the gravity of the situation.

I sensed that some sort of decision had been made by the doctors taking care of me while I was being poked and prodded. I thought that a little levity might ease the tension that was engulfing the air like debris in a twister.

"The doctors want to admit you to the hospital overnight for observation, to make sure that everything is OK," my mom told me.

At the time, I thought that was my only piece of good news. I was already rather exhausted, and didn't want to deal with anything else, including having to drive back home twenty minutes to Lindenhurst.

"That's all that they really told me," my mom said. "They want to keep you overnight for observation."

Suddenly, my mom remembered something else.

"Oh, wait!" my mom continued, "There is something else that the doctor wanted to add. Take a deep breath."

"Just tell me," I interjected impatiently.

"Because all of the hospital beds in the internal medicine ward were already occupied, the doctor told me that you would have to stay in the pediatric wing overnight."

"The pediatric wing? Are they kidding me? I'm twenty-one years old, for Christ's sake! They want to keep me in Pediatrics?"

I was a twenty-one year old, grown man...soon to be twenty-two years old...and a third year medical student. I could not believe they wanted to put me in the same ward as all of the little children I had been working with for the last six weeks. Could they possibly be serious?

I was left with the unmistakable impression that I was not being taken seriously. Perhaps had I been taken more seriously, I could have received more prompt attention when the time ultimately came, so that I did not end up with the degree of damage I have had to endure ever since. Then again, perhaps the degree of attention I received while in the pediatric ward actually was adequate. Something deep within my gut, though, tells me that this was not the case. In the end, I may never know for certain.

As I thought to myself whether or not I should complain about the condition of the care...or lack of care...that I was to receive, I tried to put a few things into their proper perspective.

First, the bicycle accident took place around 7:00 PM on Wednesday, August 13, along my bicycle ride back from Bethpage State Park. Next, I had been stuck in Mid-Island Hospital in Bethpage from around 8:00 PM until almost midnight of the following morning. That meant I had been in the hospital for at least four hours already...without a single bite to eat either!

Around 11:00 PM that night the doctors had decided that I ought to be admitted to Mid-Island Hospital for observation. I was tired, and my mom was probably even more tired. Let us not forget that I still had to study for my exam in Pediatrics that Friday as well. My exam was less than two days away. I had to study. At least, if I were in a hospital bed, I should have time to study.

Thankfully, at least, my mom didn't have to drive tomorrow the hour or so to her job as junior high school math and science teacher at Intermediate School 192 in St. Albans, Queens. Normally, that would take my mom anywhere from forty minutes to over an hour to drive to, depending upon traffic. School was out for the summer, though. My mom just had to drive the twenty-or-so minutes back to their home, and get ready for bed.

Of course, as I was going through all these calculations in my mind, I had completely forgotten about my father who was still lying in agony at the HIP Medical Center in Syosset, about fifteen minutes away in Bethpage.

When it all came down to it, the bottom line was this: If the doctors thought that I should stay overnight in the hospital, then I was staying in the hospital. If the only beds available were in the pediatric ward, then I was staying in the pediatric ward. That was it.

Without further argument or complaint, the hospital attendant took me up to the pediatric ward, while my mom drove the twenty-or-so minute drive home from Mid-Island Hospital to my parents' home. I washed up, brushed my teeth, got ready for bed, and finally went to bed…such as it was. At least, I already had my hospital gown on. The emergency room physician had already seen to that. I just wanted to sleep.

My biking clothes had been mutilated almost beyond recognition by the collision. I didn't care about my biking clothes anymore. I never did learn what ever happened to my bicycle, the bicycle helmet, or the water bottle attached to my bicycle. I didn't care about any of these things either. I just wanted to sleep.

Within five minutes, I was out like a light.

CHAPTER SEVEN

The lyrics of the song I knew
Were just not quite correct
The lyrics should have been instead
A little more like this:
"Both say a prayer for me now,
And save one for the morning after."

I awoke the following day to the screams of some dark, primal terror coming from outside the room.

"What was THAT!?" I thought. "What the hell was that?"

Somebody was dying. Of this I was certain. But who? It wasn't either my mom or dad. My mom's screams were lower in pitch...perhaps an alto or contralto. This scream was much higher in pitch. My dad didn't scream. He just yelled. These wails were not coming from either one of them...they were coming from someone else.

I recognized these God-awful sounds as the blood-curdling screams of a child in abject horror, but had no clue where the screams were coming from. All the children in my family were fully grown. There were no children in our family any longer.

"No, no!" the screams continued.

Suddenly, a light went on in my drowsy mind, and I recognized the sound as the scream of some poor child unaware of the secret purpose of the hospital's phlebotomist. That was when I remembered where I was:

Welcome to the wonderful world of real-life pediatrics at Mid-Island Hospital.

The wonderful world of real-life pediatrics was more than just playing with children and dealing with parents. The real world of pediatrics was drawing blood from terrified children who had no idea why these brutish adults were sticking them with needles. I should have known better.

As I lay there in my strange, new bed, pondering about screaming children and the real world of pediatrics, suddenly I remembered what I wasn't doing. I wasn't studying pediatrics for my pediatrics exam. My pediatrics exam was now just one day away. I had to study for my pediatrics exam.

There was just one small problem. I couldn't study for my pediatrics exam. All of my notes, handouts, and textbooks for pediatrics were at my parents' home…about a twenty minutes' drive from this room I found myself in. Twenty minutes might as well have been an eternity. I had no books. I had no car. Instead of studying, I was stuck in the hospital…in a pediatric ward, no less…without a single textbook that I could study from.

The date was now Thursday, August 14, 1991…the morning after my bicycle accident. What time was it? At last, I checked my watch on my left hand to read the time…only to discover that the glass cover of the watch had been smashed beyond recognition. The watch face was frozen at 7:28. The watch had met its maker at the exact time of the accident...never to be resurrected again. Time for a new watch...

"Oh, well," I said to no one in particular, "I guess this watch has seen its better days. This watch won't ever tell the time again."

The sounds of terrified tykes seemed to have subsided. I figured that the phlebotomist must have done his dirty deeds for the day and moved on.

I looked around the room to see if there was a wall clock anywhere in the room. I found a wall clock hanging just to the right of the entrance. The clock on the wall read about 07:30 AM.

Normally, the fact that I read the clock on the wall would not have been a big deal...certainly nothing to write home about. I had been telling the time since the age of two. This was not a normal situation, however.

Before my accident, I had perfect vision out of both eyes. In fact, I could see from twenty feet away what the average person could only see from ten feet away. I had been telling time almost as long as there were watches to tell time with. On this first day after my accident, I still had perfect vision...out of my right eye, at least...and could still tell time.

I mention that now because two months from now, upon awakening for the first time from my coma, that will no longer be true. My vision will be dramatically altered...and not for the better. Over eight months at three institutions will pass before anybody bothers to check my vision.

I cannot fault the folks at the first institution, Mid-Island Hospital. I simply wasn't conscious long enough to warrant testing. Nor can I fault the folks at the third institution, Brunswick Hospital. The physician at that hospital was the one to recommend ophthalmology evaluate me for glasses. My ire is reserved for the folks at Hillcrest Head Injury Recovery Association.

For four months of what was supposed to be rehabilitation at Hillcrest Head Injury Recovery Association, not a single doctor or therapist thought to check my vision. Had anyone bothered, that person would have soon seen that, on account of my accident, I now needed corrective lenses to reverse a newly-acquired near-sightedness.

Oh, well. That would soon be more troubled water under an already teetering bridge. Back to my story...

After checking the time, I turned my attention to my pediatric textbooks that were nowhere in sight. All of my books were at my parents' house gathering dust while I was stuck in Mid-Island Hospital. My exam was tomorrow. It was an intellectual catastrophe. How was I supposed to magically transport my pediatrics textbooks here so that I could study for my pediatrics exam? The physicians who had abandoned me in the pediatric ward may not have thought my situation all that serious, but I knew better. I had to take my pediatrics exam tomorrow. That meant I had to study.

As I sat there in my bed, wondering how I was going to study for my pediatrics exam without any textbooks, I was pleasantly interrupted by the sound of a hospital attendant handing out the morning's fare.

"Breakfast is ready," the cheery, yet pleasingly plump hospital attendant announced as she handed me my morning fare.

"Thank you," I replied.

I sat up in my bed and pondered the fare before me.

Breakfast this morning consisted of three slices of French toast, three medium, scrambled eggs, three slices of bacon, three medium sausages, some lightly toasted bread, butter, orange marmalade, orange juice and coffee with two sugar packets and three containers of Half-and half.

Normally, I would have complained about the food in front of me. "What are you trying to do with Fatone's feast of high-fat, high-cholesterol food?" I would say. "Are you trying to give me a heart attack or something?"

Normally, I would have complained about the accommodations now in front of me, except for the fact that I hadn't eaten since around lunchtime on the previous day. In the commotion surrounding the bicycle accident and my ordeals at the hospital last night, I missed out on dinner completely. Now, my stomach was growling like a grizzly bear waking up after a long hibernation. Therefore, I quit my complaining, held my nose, and ate this slop here as quickly as I could.

I ate most of my breakfast, and then got up and went to the bathroom. I brushed my teeth with the toothbrush they provided.. After brushing my teeth, I returned to my bed, elevated the head of the bed...using the electronic device situated on the side of the bed so that the head of the bed was almost vertical...and then sat up in the bed.

The time was now about 9:15 in the morning. Using the phone so thoughtfully provided at the side of my bed, I called my mom in Lindenhurst. My mom picked up on the third ring, as she always did when she was at home.

"Hi, mom," I said, "It's your son, Meme!"

"Good morning, Meme. How did you sleep last night?" my mom asked.

"Like a rock," I replied. "I sure got one hell of a wake-up call this morning, though. I woke up to the sounds of some small child screaming bloody murder because the phlebotomist was trying to draw first blood. What a wake-up call that was!"

"By the way," I continued, "Before you have to ask, I'll just go right out and tell you: No, nobody has checked in on me since last night."

"Did you honestly expect things to be different?" my mom asked.

"Well, one can always dream, can't one?"

"Oh, by the way," I continued, "On the bookcase in my bedroom... on the top shelf...was the big, green book entitled 'Nelson's Textbook of Pediatrics'. Do you know which book I mean?"

"Yes," she replied, "I think I know which book you're talking about."

"Great! Could you take this book to me while I'm stuck here in the Pediatrics ward so that I can get some studying for my upcoming exam tomorrow?"

"No problem! I'll personally hand-deliver the textbook so that you can study."

My mom and I spoke for a little while longer...about silly stuff, such as who was feeding Buffy while I was in the hospital...and serious stuff...like who was going to tell dad about what happened to me yesterday. After talking for a little while longer, I said my goodbyes to my mom, and hung up the phone.

There I was in the pediatric ward at Mid-Island Hospital. The time must have been around 9:30 AM by now. As I saw it, I had been abandoned in the pediatric ward at Mid-Island Hospital with nothing else to do. My mom would not be getting me my pediatrics books for at least a half hour or so. I didn't know what else to do. Therefore, I decided to take full advantage of the phone service provided, and call my friend, Rich. If I was lucky, I figured, perhaps I would catch him before he left his apartment to go to work at the dental school at Stony Brook, or parasailing on the Long Island Sound off of Stony Brook.

Rich was the second-year dental student whom I had tutored in pathology and a few other courses last year. Rich was a good-looking, up and coming dental student, just a little shorter than me. He had short, spiky, dirty-blonde hair that was sun-bleached from summers of wind sailing and parasailing. He had a thin, but athletic build that stood just a little shorter than me. He had deeply inset eyes, prominent, bushy, dirty-brown eyebrows, and a slightly protuberant jaw line. Back when he was in dental school, Rich was considered the dental student most likely to be wearing shorts and a Ron-Jon surfer T-shirt during summer... unless he was in clinic. Rich was a person who had to overcome major obstacles himself to be where he was.

Rich's story starts in elementary school in Woodmere, on the southwestern corner of Nassau County. Woodmere was not that far from St. Albans, Queens, where my mom used to teach junior high school math and science. Only three or so miles separated St. Albans in Queens from Woodmere in Nassau County. Socioeconomically speaking, however, the two villages were worlds apart. St. Albans in Queens was a lower-class, poor, predominantly Black district in New York City. Woodmere in Nassau County was an upper-class, affluent, predominantly Jewish enclave just outside of New York City.

When Rich was in elementary school in Woodmere, he was having great difficulty keeping up with his peers. Rich's first-grade teacher didn't understand why Rich was falling behind the other students in his class. The administrators at his school didn't understand why Rich was falling behind the other students in his class. Rich was falling behind, and his parents didn't know why either. The administrators at his school in Woodmere assumed that Rich was mentally retarded, and put Rich in special education.

Special education is a euphemistic term applied to children who, for one reason or another, did not seem to fit into the standard educational model. Children who were consigned to special education often included, in addition to mentally retarded children afflicted by conditions such as Down syndrome, any child with conduct disorders, blindness, deafness, and all manners of neurological conditions such as Tourette's syndrome. Special education was the place where students were consigned when the teachers didn't know where a student should be placed; special education was not something that people aspired to.

Early on in his elementary school career, then, on account of Rich's failure to keep up with the rest of the children in his class, he was placed in special education along with all of the blind, deaf and mentally retarded children, as well as the children with conduct disorders and all manners of neurological conditions.

Not surprisingly, special education did not smile down upon poor, little Rich. Special education did not appear to agree with Rich at all. Rich began to complain…as best a six-year-old child could complain about anything…to his parents about his current predicament.

As Rich began to complain more verbally about his predicament, Rich's parents became increasingly concerned with the quality of his education. Rich's parents sought out various specialists in the hope of identifying the nature of Rich's scholastic difficulties. Finally, one of the specialists correctly identified Rich's problem, and communicated his findings to Rich's parents. Rich's parents, in turn, explained to the teachers and administrators at Rich's elementary school in Woodmere why Rich was having trouble in school: Rich, it turned out, had dyslexia.

Dyslexia is part of a host of neurological conditions that impact how people see and/or hear the world around them. Blindness is one of the more obvious such neurological conditions; blind people cannot see the world around. Deafness is another such neurological condition; deaf people cannot hear the world around them. Dyslexia, in a way, is a neurological condition not at all that dissimilar from blindness or deafness.

Dyslexia is a condition that occurs where people don't process written letters the way you or I normally process written letters. You or I might see the word "letters" written down on a page, and know the symbols to represent "letters." Rich, on the other hand, when shown the same word, "letters," written down on a page, might see "estrelt" or "retstel" instead. To Rich, these letters simply had no meaning; they were just meaningless symbols on a page.

If, on the other hand, instead of writing down the words and asking him to repeat the words, you told him to repeat the word "letters," he would hear the word correctly as "letters", and reply correctly with the word "letters". Were he in a good mood, he might even put the word in a sentence. For a person with dyslexia, speech and hearing were never the problem per se. For the person with dyslexia, the written word was the enemy. That was what it meant to be dyslexic. That was what Rich was suffering from…dyslexia.

Finally, the teachers and administrators learned what Rich was suffering from: Rich had dyslexia. Once the appropriate diagnosis had been made, appropriate modifications were then made to better suit his problem. With appropriate accommodations for his dyslexia that included using a reader to speak the questions to him, Rich was able to break free from the bonds of special education and resume a reasonably normal education with his peers.

Not only did Rich successfully graduate from elementary, junior high, and high school, but Rich then went on to college. In fact, Rich graduated from college, and went on to study dentistry at SUNY Stony Brook, a dental school ranked second, according to at least one survey of the thirty-or-so dental schools in the United States. Rich didn't do all that bad for himself after all.

I first met Rich in the fall of 1990, while I was a second-year medical student at Stony Brook. Rich was an incoming, first-year dental student. When I first met Rich, Rich was having trouble with some of his coursework. Rich told me that he was having trouble with pathology, one of the courses medical and dental students took together.

"No problem!" I said. "I took Pathology two years ago…and I got honors in that course. Do you want me to help you in Pathology?"

"Can you?"

"No problem! I can be your Pathology tutor. Besides, by tutoring you in pathology, I'll get practice for the pathology section of Step One of the National Board of Medical Examiners licensing exam."

Tutoring Rich in Pathology was definitely one reason I ended up scoring as well as I did on Step One of the National Board of Medical Examiners licensing exam. For that I will remain forever grateful to Rich.

I became Rich's tutor for pathology, microbiology, and genetics. Rich and I hit it off well, and ended up becoming friends. Even though Rich was in the class after me, Rich was actually a year older than me. I didn't care about that though, and neither did he. Thanks to a successful tutoring partnership, I helped Rich to pass his pathology, microbiology, and genetics classes that spring.

When I needed to take a break from medical school during that semester…feeling burnt out from all the long, grueling hours of studying…Rich and I simply packed our textbooks into my shiny, economical, white 1989 Volkswagen Fox/Polo and drove the twenty-two hours from Stony Brook to Melbourne, Florida, to visit with my sister, Vaia. After staying with my sister for two days of sun and tennis, and a one-day holiday excursion to the Walt Disney World Epcot Center in nearby Orlando, Rich and I drove back the twenty-two-or-so hours to Stony Brook. Rich passed that test in microbiology as well.

On that morning of August 14, 1991, after calling my mom about my pediatrics books, I called Rich at his apartment in Stony Brook. Nobody picked up. Thinking that, if I couldn't speak to Rich himself, I could at least speak with Rich's parents, Lois and Marvin, I called Rich at his parents' house in Woodmere.

Rich's mom picked up the phone.

"Richman residence…how can I help you?" Mrs. Richman answered.

"Hi, Mrs. Richman, this is Demetrius. Could you tell me where Rich is?" I replied.

"Hi, Demetrius! Sure, Rich is in his room. I'll get him."

Mrs. Richman put the phone down, and called out to Rich: "Rich, Demetrius is on the other line. Pick up!"

From the other line, one could hear the sound of a second line being picked up.

"Rich?" I asked.

"OK mom! I got it!" Rich yelled to his mom. Through the telephone, I could hear the sound of the first line letting go.

"Hello, Rich? Guess what! You're not going to believe what happened to me last night. Guess where I am!" I started.

"Where?"

"I'm in Mid-Island Hospital in Bethpage! I was admitted last night."

"You were where? Why?"

I then told Rich the short story about my bicycle accident. I told Rich how I was struck yesterday evening by another bike, and flipped over my bicycle and landed head first on the pavement. I told Rich how I had a splitting headache after somersaulting onto the pavement, while the other cyclist, who hit me, landed on the grass, and basically was fine.

"Oh, there was one more thing that I forgot to mention yesterday, while talking the doctors and other people...including the paramedics," I continued. "The whole time this accident took place, I was wearing my helmet. The other bicyclist…the guy who hit me…wasn't wearing a helmet."

"Are you serious?" Rich asked, incredulously. I was sure that, had Rich been there, he would have been scratching his head in bemusement.

"You better believe I'm serious." I told him.

I then proceeded to tell Rich some of the highlights of my journey from Bethpage State Parkway, where I had my accident, to Mid-Island Hospital in Bethpage.

"After I had my fall, a passerby who saw the accident asked me if I was alright, and if I needed an ambulance. I told the person that I felt a little shaky, and thought it best if I got checked out. Therefore, the passerby called for an ambulance."

"Sometime after the accident…I suppose that it could have been either five minutes or fifty minutes, because at that point, I had absolutely no concept of time…the ambulance arrived, and the paramedic came out from the vehicle to check me out. Upon seeing what had happened to me, the paramedic decided that I should be taken to the nearest hospital…which in this case was Mid-Island Hospital in Bethpage."

"Once in Mid-Island Hospital, I was checked out by an emergency room doc. Next, I was taken to radiology to have some X-rays and, I believe, a CAT scan. I also had my blood drawn. Finally, around midnight, the powers that be decided that I should be admitted overnight for observation. Therefore, here I am."

"Oh, wait…there was one more thing." I told Rich. "Because all of beds in internal medicine were already taken…or so they said, at any rate…I had to stay overnight in the pediatric ward instead of the internal medicine ward, even though I was, after all, twenty-one years old…soon to be twenty-two years old."

"What? Are you kidding me?" Rich exclaimed. Rich was absolutely incredulous at the thought that I was in the pediatric ward. Rich was never one to hide his true feelings.

"What's wrong with these people?" Rich added.

I tried to calm Rich down by saying to him some of the same things that my mom told me earlier last night, but feared that he was even less convinced than I was when my mom told me the same things last night.

"This doesn't sound right," Rich started. "Do you want the name of a good lawyer? I actually know a few good lawyers. I am sure that these people would be more than happy to help you out. They can even waive some of their usual fees, since I'll tell them that you are a good friend of mine."

"Maybe later," I said. "For now, I still have to study for my upcoming exam in pediatrics…which I am supposed to take tomorrow morning at Stony Brook. Don't worry about it. We'll talk more about getting compensated for any damages I may have suffered on account of this bicycle accident."

At that time, I did not think that I had much cause to seek compensation. Now…after having witnessed all the acts of gross negligence and outright incompetence I suffered at the hands of certain physicians and paraprofessionals…I wish I had taken Rich up on his offer to hire a lawyer right then and there.

"I've got a few errands to run this morning," Rich said finally, "But I'll stop by after I am done. Sound good?"

"Sounds good to me," I replied. "In the meantime, I'll just sit tight and wait for my mom to come with my pediatrics books so I can study some for my test."

"Alright. Bye!"

Rich and I said our goodbyes, and then hung up the phone. I started to get out of bed to change into my clothes when I stopped dead in my tracks.

"You big dummy," I exclaimed to nobody in particular, "What are you thinking?" 'Big dummy' was an alternative to some of the more colorful expletives that I felt added little to situations such as these.

"Where do you think you are going?" I berated myself. "Aren't you forgetting something? Somebody is wearing a hospital gown because somebody's clothes were mutilated in a little bicycle accident! Somebody is not going anywhere."

I had forgotten. I had changed out of my mutilated bicycle clothes, and into my hospital gown. I didn't have any clothes except for this hospital gown with its gaping hole over the derrière. I wouldn't be going anywhere...anytime soon.

As I lay at the edge of my bed pondering my absolute lack of any appropriate attire, my mom entered the room with what appeared to be my pediatric textbook.

"Hi, mom," I greeted my mom, "You made it here fast!"

"Hi!" my mom replied. "Traffic wasn't too bad now. How are you feeling today? How do you like your new surroundings?"

"Well, the headache seems to have gone away completely. Unfortunately, my cuts and bruises have not been so quick to heal. Even the bruising appears...at least to me the last time that I checked in the mirror...to have gone down a little, although I suppose I could just be imagining that part. I do believe we have to do something about my garment of choice."

I pointed to a piece of naked flesh popping out of my hospital gown just above the derriere.

"I'm glad your headache is gone," my mom replied. "I can't say much about the accoutrements!"

"I do have to say, though, that the general ambience of this pediatric ward does leave something to be desired," I told my mom.

I then told my mom about my special privilege of awakening to the sounds of screaming small-fries…terror-stricken at the sight of needles being stuck in their arms by the brutish phlebotomist at the pediatric ward.

"I have to tell you," I told my mom. "The agony and terror in these children gave me serious pause about becoming a pediatrician."

"I can understand your reservations after witnessing the real world of pediatrics, but do try to remember one thing, though," my mom reminded me, "You can still make a real difference in a child's life as a thoughtful, caring pediatrician. I wouldn't give up on pediatrics quite so quickly simply on account of a few screaming children. I'd wait and see what you think of all the other specialties as well. Besides, who knows, maybe you will end up interested in surgery instead!"

"That's true. Don't worry about that. The way I see it, I have at least a year to figure out what field looks the most interesting to me. Until that time, I intend to treat every field…whether pediatrics, family medicine, surgery, obstetrics & gynecology, psychiatry or medicine… as if that's the field I may end up going into."

I wasn't lying about what I was saying. At that time, I truly did not know which field I ultimately would enter. Every field of medical training looked inviting…with the sole exception of psychiatry, which I had generally considered voodoo medicine. As I saw it, psychiatry was never, and would never become for me an acceptable medical alternative.

"By the way," my mom said, "I hope I got the right book for you to read."

My mom then handed me the green textbook entitled, "Nelson's Textbook of Pediatrics." It was the right medical textbook.

"Great!" I replied. "That's just the book I wanted. At last I will finally have something that I can read for my exam tomorrow at Stony Brook. Now I suppose I will have at least a chance of doing well on my pediatric exam. Thanks!"

I thanked my mom for bringing me the textbook, and promised my mom that I would study from that book as soon as my mom left.

"You know, mom," I told my mom in a somewhat more subdued tone, "One thing has gotten me a little worried, though. It's now around ten o'clock in the morning...and, so far, I haven't seen either hide or hair of this elusive internal medicine team that was supposed to take care of me. It's like the team got lost somewhere on the way to the pediatric ward, and never got home."

"I mean, I have absolutely no idea what happened to the medical team," I continued. "I've been up and about for at least the last two-and-a-half hours, and so far nobody at all has come to talk to me, examine me, or even just say 'Hi!' I mean absolutely nobody. The only person who actually did come by so far this morning...so that he could draw my blood...was the phlebotomist who, by the way, seemed more than a little grateful that I was not just another screaming, tortured child crying for his or her mommy. I suppose that, if I were the phlebotomist, I would thank God for small favors."

The problem, as I saw it, was that, once again, it appeared that I was not being taken seriously as a patient. I did not know the reason for the apparent oversight. Did somebody think that I did not deserve to be admitted to the hospital? Were there perhaps other, more needy patients who required my attention?

I look upon that unfortunate oversight now with some degree of sadness and anger. I say anger because the whole time between the accident and the impending seizure I was doing everything I was supposed to be doing. I was in a hospital...admitted for observation so that, were something to go wrong, I could be afforded the sort of prompt medical care needed to improve my odds of survival. I also say anger because precious time was wasted on worthless inactivity in the pediatric ward.

On the other hand, I say sadness when I realize that, had I only been more insistent on being monitored in a medical rather than pediatric ward, I could have ensured the more careful attention that just might have averted the impending catastrophe. Instead of being more insistent on receiving the proper medical attention, I merely marveled to my mom over the apparent inactivity of the physicians in whose care I had currently found myself.

Just as I was talking to my mother, the entire medical team, including the attending physician, two resident physicians, a nurse, and a social worker, converged at the entrance to my room. After first conversing amongst themselves...words that were, alas, completely inaudible to me...the entire team entered my room. The attending physician introduced himself.

"Hello! My name is Dr. Nicolletti. I am the neurologist assigned to your case. How are you feeling today?" the attending physician asked. "I hear you had quite the little fall last night...while riding your bicycle, I guess?"

Dr. Nicolletti was a tall, middle-aged physician. He stood about six feet tall, and had salt-and-pepper hair. He appeared in reasonable shape. He was neither obese nor emaciated. He also had a deep, baritone voice that seemed to soothe all with whom he spoke.

"I guess you might say that I had a little fender-bender last night with my bicycle" I started. "I assume you want the short version, rather than the long version of the story."

I then proceeded for the third time in two days with the short version of my story. "Yesterday evening," I began, "My bicycle collided with another bicycle on the bicycle trail along Bethpage State Parkway. Upon colliding, I flipped over my bicycle and landed head-first on the pavement."

"Oh," I added, almost as an afterthought, "I should also mention that I was in fact wearing my helmet when I had my accident, and did not take off my helmet until after the accident." This apparent afterthought would prove of much greater significance later on than when first speaking to the neurologist.

"That's good. I agree. Wearing a helmet is very important," Dr. Nicolletti replied. Dr. Nicolletti then turned to face me more directly. "Now, let me take a look at you to make sure everything is OK," Dr. Nicolletti said.

Dr. Nicolletti bent over a little to examine my head more closely. After examining my head more closely, Dr. Nicolletti turned his attention to the two resident physicians in the team who had stood silently up to this point.

"What do you think of the ecchymosis surrounding the orbital areas?" Dr. Nicolletti then asked the resident physicians.

"Oh, I can answer that!" I replied. "Besides just being a patient, I am, after all, a third-year medical student myself. I have both a personal and a professional interest in this case. I've also had a chance to take a real good look at myself. I relish the chance to contribute to this discussion in a meaningful way."

I thought that I knew a little something about my own situation. I felt I should share this with the doctors taking care of me. I wasn't being boastful or condescending to anyone. I just wanted to feel like I was contributing to my own treatment in a meaningful way.

I continued: "There is bruising in the skin and subdermal spaces around both eye sockets that is more marked on the left than on the right side. The left eye is almost completely obstructed by the weight of the bruising above the left eye. I should also note that my vision overall, so far, has not been affected by the bruising. In addition, upon lifting the left eyelid, one sees several prominent red splotches in the sclera of the left eye…as well as a few smaller red splotches in the sclera of the right eye."

"That's not bad." Dr. Nicolletti replied. "Is there anything anybody would like to add to this?"

"Oh, I should also mention," I continued, "I have various cuts, scrapes and bruises on my legs, arms and face, as well as in my hair. I also think that I have a pretty big bump, on my head from the fall. I had a pretty bad headache yesterday evening, but the headache seems to have gone away now."

"OK…that's fine. I'm glad the headache has gone away. Does anybody else have anything to add?" Dr. Nicolletti asked.

Nobody else had anything to add at the moment.

"Alright, then," Dr. Nicolletti continued as he turned once again to face me and my mom, "Here's the situation as I see things so far. You have had pretty bad bruising to your face and head…not to mention your arms and legs. We are going to keep an eye on them. In the meantime, I have ordered some tests to make sure that everything was OK. Those test results should come back later this afternoon. If these test results come back, and everything looks OK, then I will send you home. Until that time, just sit tight and wait."

As Dr. Nicolletti left the room, he turned back to face me and my mom, and asked: "Do either one of you have any questions for me?"

"No," I replied, "I think I'm good for now."

"I'm fine," my mom replied.

"I'll leave you for now," Dr. Nicolletti replied as he began to leave the room, "Remember, if the test results come back, and everything looks alright, then I should be able to send you home later today."

If only that had actually been the case...and all of the tests returned back negative...all of my problems would have been solved, and I would have been returned safely to my mom in Lindenhurst. If only it had been truly so...

With that, the entire medical team shuffled off to their next patient, leaving me alone with my mom.

I turned back to my mom, and continued with some more small talk. As I was talking with my mom, Rich entered the room from the hallway outside.

"Hey, 'Metri!" he waved. "How's the sickie?" As Rich entered the room more fully, he realized that my mom was still in the room. Rich turned to address my mom. "Hi, Mrs. Moutsiakis, how are you?"

"Funny you should mention that, Rich" my mom replied. "Considering that my husband just told me that he was dying a slow and painful death at the HIP Medical Center in Syosset, about fifteen minutes north of here, and now my son is lying here in Mid-Island Hospital, in Bethpage...I guess I'd say that I'm about as good as can be expected given the circumstances that I'm under."

Rich then shook hands with my mom.

"That reminds me," my mom continued, turning now more to face me than Rich, "I should probably drive to the HIP Medical Center in Syosset to see if your father is fine, or if I should call our priest, Father Max, to say the last rites for my father yet again. Don't worry...I'll be sure to let your father know what happened to you, and I'll give your father your love from Mid-Island Hospital."

With that, my mom said her goodbyes to me and Rich, and then drove off the fifteen-or-so minutes' drive to the HIP medical center in Syosset to visit my dying father who would, apparently, escape death once again.

"So what did your doctors have to say," Rich began. "I assume that you spoke to the doctors."

"Actually," I replied, "the whole team was just there a little while ago...the attending physician, residents, nurses...the whole team. Basically, Dr. Nicolletti, the attending physician told me that he was waiting for some test results to come back. If the test results come back good, and there aren't any more issues, then he can send me home later today. In the meantime, I'm just sitting here in the pediatric ward... waiting for these test results to come back."

"That doesn't sound all that bad. It sounds like everything is under control. Don't forget, when you get out of the hospital, we have to have a rematch of that last tennis game of ours. I mean...come on...you killed me last time. You have to give me a chance for a rematch!"

"I haven't forgotten."

"Don't forget, either," Rich continued, "My offer to hook you up with those attorney-friends of mine still stands. All you have to do is to say the word, and I can have my seven savage Jewish lawyers converge upon this place faster than you can say 'settlement'. Think about it!"

Hearing of the seven savage Jewish lawyers converging on Mid-Island, I couldn't control myself. I burst out laughing.

"Hey!" Rich protested. "I'm being serious here! Think about it."

"I'm sorry, Rich," I replied, barely able to regain my composure after the thought of seven savage Jewish lawyers converging upon Mid-Island Hospital. "I'll take that under advisement."

After talking for a little while longer, mostly about small stuff of no great importance, Rich left. Shortly after Rich left, another hospital attendant appeared, and handed me a lunch tray. Lunch was served.

Lunch did not prove nearly as appetizing as breakfast…which wasn't all that appetizing to begin with. Perhaps the reason for this discrepancy was the fact that, at breakfast, I was basically starving to death, while by lunch, I was less hungry. As a result, I was more selective with lunch than breakfast.

Lunch consisted of a ham and cheese sandwich on bleached-white bread, a small container of potato salad swimming in oil, some mysterious meat dish with browned potatoes, and black coffee with two creamers and two packets of sugar. I finished as much of lunch as I could stomach.

I couldn't procrastinate any longer. I had talked to Rich for at least an hour. Rich was now gone. I had talked to my mom. My mom had brought my pediatric textbook to me. My mom was now gone. There would be no more procrastinating. I opened up Nelson's <u>Textbook of Pediatrics</u>, and began to study for my upcoming exam.

I flipped ahead to the section on rheumatic fever. That particular section was already highlighted in orange and yellow…sure signs that I had read this section at least twice before. I began re-reading that section again.

Sometime after two o'clock, my mom returned to check up on me.

"Hi, Meme!" my mom greeted me.

"Hi, mom! What's up?" I replied.

"I just thought I'd check up on you again before heading down to Jack La Lane for some exercise…to burn off some steam. How have you been? Has anybody come by to check up on you since Dr. Nicolletti came by earlier?"

"I'm OK. I've just been studying for my exam tomorrow...mostly just going over the same stuff again and again so that things stay fresh for the exam. Rich left. Nobody else has stopped by to tell me if I will be staying or if I'm gone. In the meantime, I've just been studying my pediatrics."

My mom and I chatted for a little while longer...mostly about the small stuff.

"As soon as I get the OK," I told my mom, "I'll call home for you to pick me up. Oh...by the way, you might want to pick me up some shorts, a T-shirt, and some sandals. If I try to leave the hospital dressed like this, they just might admit me to the Psych ward!"

"Call me as soon as you get the OK. If I'm not home," my mom said, "Don't panic. That just means that I'm at Jack La Lane. Just leave a message, and as soon as I get home, I'll drop my stuff off and then pick you up. I'll also bring a fresh change of clothes from your room."

"Sounds good to me. Just go to Jack. I'll be fine!"

"OK, I'm going already!"

I watched my mom leave, and then turned back to Nelson's Textbook of Pediatrics. I thumbed back to the section on rheumatic fever, and continued reading.

There I was...sitting up in bed and studying Nelson's textbook of Pediatrics on the pediatric ward in Mid Island Hospital...when it happened.

The other shoe dropped.

The details for the next two months get a little fuzzy.

I remember trying to study pediatrics when my headache, which had pretty much gone away last night, came back with a vengeance. My head was splitting harder than a log split open by Davey Crockett himself.

I don't know if anyone gave me Tylenol, aspirin, or any of the non-steroidal anti-inflammatory drugs commonly referred to as NSAIDs to try to combat my headache. I certainly hope not.

There are a few things that every medical student or aspiring physician should know. For example, don't pour salt on an open wound unless one likes experiencing pain. Never combine bleach products with ammonia products unless one likes to burn a person's lungs.

Another equally important medical but slightly less well-known axiom is the following: If a person is actively bleeding, whether from the gums, from the gut, or in this case from an arterial bleed in the epidural space, and complains of a headache, do not, under any circumstances, give that person a drug such as Tylenol or, worse still, aspirin.

Tylenol, or for that matter any of the non-steroidal anti-inflammatory drugs commonly known as NSAIDs, cause the tiny cells in the blood called platelets, which normally stick together to form clots, to no longer stick together and form clots. When platelets cannot stick together and form clots to plug any holes in the blood vessel walls, the blood and all of its contents leak into the surrounding tissues. People bleed to death.

Tylenol is bad enough… the platelets can't form clots for about six hours. Aspirin is even worse than Tylenol because the platelets of people who take aspirin are permanently knocked out; it takes up to five days for new platelets to form. Giving me either drug…either aspirin or Tylenol…would have been bad, because both drugs interfere with my ability to form clots, and would have made the epidural bleed that I was having even worse.

I did remember one thing as I lay in bed…in too much pain to continue studying. My headache kept getting worse, much worse. What had started as a minor inconvenience soon escalated into what would become the worst headache of my life. I couldn't read. I couldn't study. The pounding ache in my head had my full attention.

There I was…lying in agony in the pediatric ward. Finally, just when I thought things couldn't get any worse, it happened. I had my first and only seizure. My light went out. Nobody was home. This was my only seizure I ever had…to be sure…but it was a good seizure…a seizure that would land me in a coma…or semi-coma…for the next two months.

One thing was now abundantly clear…lying unattended in the pediatric ward. I wouldn't be in pediatrics much longer.

CHAPTER EIGHT

Tick-tock, tick-tock...tempus fugit.
Tick-tock, tick-tock...time went by.
I just watched, almost transfixed,
As my whole life ebbed by

On August 14, 1991, sometime around three in the afternoon...I don't believe anyone truly knows what time exactly except for the Father, the Son and the Holy Spirit...I had my first and only seizure. I had my seizure at exactly the place where I felt I should have been safest...in a hospital.

I didn't have my seizure anywhere. I had my seizure while an inpatient in the pediatric ward of Mid Island Hospital...ignoring for the moment the fact that, at twenty-one years of age, I was significantly older than the normal eighteen-year-old cut-off that marked the transition from pediatrics to medicine. I was still an inpatient in the pediatric ward despite the fact that traumatic brain injury was a very serious condition that would require the medical staff's full attention. Somebody felt that my situation could be monitored safely from the comfort of a pediatric nursing station. Somebody was wrong.

I had my seizure then and there. There were several important implications of the seizure. One implication was that, at last, I would require the more immediate attention of the medical team that had banished me to the pediatric ward. Another implication was that I would not be staying in the pediatric ward very much longer.

The next two months have been permanently erased from my consciousness. It is almost as if these two months never existed. Of course, I do not really believe that the next two months did not exist simply because I was in a coma. I am not a great fool. Life went on… with or without me in it.

The events of my life for the next two months…starting with my seizure…have been pieced together from my somewhat fragmentary medical records…combined with accounts from my mom. Using these medical records that I was so thoughtfully given…provided via court order many months later…and conversations with my mom…I have pieced together the closest thing to the truth that I could find. I have tried to keep all embellishments to a minimum. What follows now is an account of events associated with the ruptured middle meningeal arterial bleed that completed the downward spiral into my coma…after the other shoe dropped.

I return you now to the pediatric ward in Mid-Island Hospital.

A licensed practical nurse…wearing a white lab coat over her sky-blue pediatric hospital scrubs with imprints of Winnie the Pooh and Tigger, too…was moving from room to room on the third-floor pediatrics ward and giving medications to the children who required them. The licensed practical nurse was a pleasant, younger-looking, light-skinned young black woman…with her curly hair set carefully within a hair net…who appeared to be fairly new to the position. I suppose that this licensed practical nurse might have been straight out of college or university.

As the licensed practical nurse approached my room, she heard some rather strange rattling noises…punctuated by occasional crashing and clattering sounds…coming from my room. The nurse became curious regarding the strange sounds emanating from my room, and decided to investigate.

Upon entering my room, the horrified licensed practical nurse discovered my disheveled body all twisted around in my hospital sheets…writhing on the floor in what were apparently grand mal convulsions. Before the nurse could do or say anything else, the nurse let out a blood-curdling scream. Without uttering a single other sound, the licensed practical nurse raced out of the room in search of somebody… anybody…who could help me as I lay writhing about on the third floor of the hospital…in the pediatric ward…having what the licensed practical nurse had correctly identified as grand mal seizures.

The licensed practical nurse ran to the nearby pediatric nurse's station just as quickly as she could. Upon reaching the nurse's station, she stopped to catch her breath. Sitting in the nurse's station in the middle of a large, cylindrical table with various workstations sprouting from every corner was a somewhat heavy-set, pale-skinned female whose identification badge indicated she was the head nurse of the pediatric ward. The licensed practical nurse had been introduced to the head nurse some time ago.

The head nurse was deep in thought, but not on account of my grand mal seizure. Rather, General Hospital, a rather popular television soap opera among female nursing staff, was playing on the compact, twelve-inch television screen in the nurse's station. The head nurse was transfixed by the action in this small screen, and not easily distracted.

The licensed practical nurse rushed to the side of the head nurse who still sat, transfixed to her compact television screen.

"Quick!" the licensed practical nurse exclaimed. "Quick! Come to Room 316! There's a patient on the floor. I think he's having a seizure, or something! Come on. Quick!"

"What!?" the head nurse asked as the head nurse turned to face the licensed practical nurse…apparently upset at the thought of this young upstart's dragging her away from an exciting new episode of <u>General Hospital</u>...a soap opera that only appeared on television between three and four o'clock in the afternoon.

"Quick," the licensed practical nurse reported a little more calmly yet insistently, "There is a patient lying on the floor in Room 316. The patient is lying on the floor partially wrapped up in the hospital sheets. It looks like he is convulsing. I think he may be having a seizure or something."

Upon hearing the words "convulsing" and "seizure", the head nurse left the world of <u>General Hospital</u> behind, and sprang forth into action.

"I'd better go and see what's going on," the head nurse said.

The head nurse practically jumped out of the rather tiny chair that had been supporting the weight of her substantially larger body, and raced toward my room, with the licensed practical nurse right on her heels. When the head nurse approached my room and came inside, the head nurse found me...writhing and convulsing on the floor...in the throes of what apparently was a full-blown, grand mal seizure. It appeared that the licensed practical nurse was correct after all.

The head nurse immediately turned to the licensed practical nurse. The head nurse was more than a little frazzled. It had been a while since the last time that the head nurse had witnessed a full-blown, grand mal seizure...certainly not in a pediatric ward...and certainly never by herself before. The head nurse paused for just a moment in order to regain her composure. After quickly regaining her composure, the head nurse said to the licensed practical nurse:

"We have to call a code." The head nurse was trying mighty hard to maintain her composure. "Call a code red...medical emergency...in the pediatric ward on the third floor. Call it now!"

The licensed practical raced back to the nurse's station, and found the intercom. Quickly, the licensed practical nurse pressed the big, red call button and spoke into the receiver just above the red button.

"Attention," the licensed practical nurse spoke over the intercom. "There is a Code Red...medical emergency...in the pediatric ward on the third floor. I repeat, Code Red...Medical Emergency...in the pediatric ward on the third floor."

The licensed practical nurse then let go of the big, red call button. The licensed practical nurse quickly wiped the sweat that was pouring from her forehead, and down the sides of her face, with a paper towel, and then tossed the paper towel in the trash. Still dripping with sweat, the licensed practical nurse wiped the sweat off once again with another paper towel as she tried mightily to maintain her composure.

The licensed practical nurse walked back to my room just a little more calmly than before. When the licensed practical nurse returned to my room just down the hallway, she found the head nurse attending to my writhing and convulsing body on the floor.

"OK," the licensed practical nurse told the head nurse, "I called the code. Help should be here in a matter of minutes."

The pediatric head nurse still lay on the floor by my body... attending to my writhing and convulsing body. The licensed practical nurse stood by the nearby window...watching the scene as it unfolded before her eyes. Both were soon joined by the pediatric chief resident, who was wearing standard-issue green, polyester scrubs partially covered up by her full-length lab coat lined with four front pockets...two on each side...jam-packed with pens, papers, pocket-sized textbooks and miscellaneous medical devices.

The pediatric chief resident saw me lying on the floor, and turned to face the pediatric head nurse and the licensed practical nurse. She spoke to them:

"Who called the code?" the pediatric chief resident wanted to know.

The pediatric head nurse replied to the pediatric chief resident: "I told her to call a code on this patient."

The pediatric chief resident appeared to be befuddled for a moment. The pediatric chief resident didn't remember taking care of any adult patients in the pediatric ward at this time. The pediatric chief looked up, and read my name from a small sign posted by the door to the room.

"That's not my patient," the pediatric chief resident told the pediatric head nurse and licensed practical nurse. "I'm the pediatric chief resident. I look after pediatric cases…in other words, children. That's not my patient. What you want is the medical service. This patient is on their service. I'd like to help, but I don't know his case at all. I'm afraid I might do more harm than good. You will have to page Medical Team B. Medical Team B is the team that is covering him."

The pediatric chief resident pointed to a blue square and the letter "B" alongside my name written on a small sign just outside the door to his room.

"Do you see this blue square with the letter 'B' next to it?" the pediatric chief resident asked. "That blue square indicates that patient is being covered by the medical service, and the letter "B" signifies Team B. I am the pediatric chief resident. You want to speak to Medical Team B."

The pediatric chief resident continued. "I'll tell you what. I'll page Medical Team B to this unit while you continue to attend to the patient. In the meantime, you just continue to care for the patient."

With that, the pediatric chief resident left the room to page Medical Team B to this floor.

The pediatric head nurse continued to attend to me while the pediatric chief resident left the room and the licensed practical nurse stood idly by, unsure what more the licensed practical nurse could do or the pediatric head nurse could ask of her.

About a minute later, the pediatric chief resident returned to my room from the pediatric nurse's station. Once again, the pediatric chief resident turned to address the pediatric head nurse, and said.

"I just paged everyone from Medical Team B to the pediatric ward on the third floor of the hospital," the pediatric chief resident reported to the pediatric head nurse. "Everybody should be down shortly."

The pediatric chief resident then turned to the licensed practical nurse, and said: "You should greet the medical team at the nurse's station so that you can direct the Medical Team to the right room."

"OK," the licensed practical nurse replied, "I can do that." With that, the licensed practical nurse left the room where I still lay writhing and convulsing in order to man the nurse's station for the impending arrival of Medical Team B.

The pediatric chief resident then turned back to the pediatric head nurse, and said: "If you have any pediatric emergencies or other issues, feel free to page me. You have my pager number. If you don't have any pediatric emergencies, then I will leave you so that I can get back to my work."

The pediatric chief resident then left to attend to the other pediatric emergencies that needed her attention at that time.

As promised, within a matter of minutes, a veritable swarm of white coats swooped down upon the pediatric ward. The medical chief resident for Team B arrived first...followed soon thereafter by the first of two junior medical residents. As the members of Medical Team B arrived at the nurse's station, the licensed practical nurse directed the team members to Room 316...the room where I still lay having my seizure.

"What is the problem?" the medical chief resident asked the pediatric head nurse as he approached Room 316.

"Well," the pediatric head nurse replied, "apparently, while handing out medications, my licensed practical nurse was worried by some strange noises coming from your room, and looked in on your patient a little while ago…only to discover that your patient was lying on the floor and having a seizure."

The concern on the face of the medical chief resident was obvious. It did not take a genius to figure out that something was wrong. The medical chief resident was no great fool.

The medical chief resident quickly assessed the situation at hand. The patient, a young white male, was on the floor, and having a grand-mal seizure. The patient was writhing, contorting himself, and frothing at the mouth.

"Somebody page Dr. Weinstein, the attending physician for Medical Team B" the medical chief resident said to no one in particular. "When he calls back, tell him that he needs to come in. Tell him that one of his patients," as the medical chief resident paused a minute to read my name from the hospital-issued wrist tag, "a Deh-Meh-Tree-Oos Moot-Sick-Ee-Ass…sorry, I can't read it…anyway, just tell Dr. Weinstein that one of his patients on the third-floor pediatrics wing is having a seizure. Tell Dr. Weinstein that he needs to come quickly."

The junior medical resident immediately went from my room back to the nurse's station to page Dr. Weinstein. While the junior resident was paging Dr, Weinstein, the medical chief resident turned and faced me in order to better assess the situation.

The situation was not improving. I still had most of the various cuts, scrapes, and bruises on my arms, legs, and face that I had earlier in the day…while first talking with the medical team. I had at least managed to wash some of the blood from my head and face off. Of course, the bruising around both eyes was still there...left side still worse that the right. If anything, the bruising pattern on the patient appeared a little more colorful now than earlier in the day. My typical black-and blue pattern was now accented with other hues like magenta, crimson and burnt umber.

More important from my point of view was the fact that I was writhing and convulsing on the floor...having a full-blown, grand mal convulsion. I was frothing at the mouth. These features added a certain air of unreality to the entire situation. The situation was not improving. If anything, the situation was getting worse.

The medical chief resident had completed his initial assessment of the situation. The first thing that the medical chief resident had to do... if he was to do anything at all...was to control the seizures. In order to control the seizures, the patient needed some valium...for me, obviously, not himself...although I suppose I would have understood his own need for valium as well.

While the medical chief resident completed his initial assessment of the situation, the first junior medical resident returned from the nurse's station, joined now by the second junior medical resident.

The medical chief resident spoke to the two junior medical residents crowding around the entrance to my room:

"We have to control this patient's seizures. We need to get some valium IM from the crash cart so that we can control his seizures," the medical chief resident said. "Go down the hall and get me the crash cart."

The medical chief resident motioned for the second junior medical resident...who was furthest from him and closest to the door...to retrieve the crash cart from down the hall. The second junior medical resident jumped at the chance to do something useful in this situation, and sprinted down the hall in search of the crash cart. The second junior medical resident quickly spotted the crash cart...interspersed amidst the clutter that defined the pediatric ward…ran to reach the cart, and quickly maneuvered the cart around the clutter and to my room.

"Here's the crash cart," the second junior medical resident said to the medical chief resident between puffs of breath. Although there were some obstacles to avoid while bringing the cart, these obstacles seemed surmountable. Perhaps the second junior medical resident could use some conditioning training himself, but that was a different matter altogether.

The medical chief resident quickly searched the cart until he spied the vial marked diazepam, the generic term for Valium. The medical chief resident then prepared to inject me with valium intramuscularly. He first shook the vial a few times. Next he took the syringe, removed the cap, inverted the vial, drew up the solution of valium from the vial into the syringe, removed any residual air bubbles in the syringe, shot me with the syringe, drew back to ensure that I was in muscle tissue rather than a blood vessel, and injected me with valium.

After injecting me with valium, the medical chief resident discarded the used syringe in the Sharps container located near the entrance to the room. The medical chief resident then passed the vial containing valium back to the second junior medical resident, and told him to first put the valium back in the crash cart, and put the crash cart back where he found it.

The medical chief resident watched me as the seizures first became weaker and less violent, and then appeared to stop altogether as the effect of the valium was made manifest. About that time, as the seizures appeared to stop, Dr. Weinstein appeared outside my room from down the hallway, decked out in bright, multi-colored, pattered shorts as if at a golf outing or summer barbeque.

"Hello, again," Dr. Weinstein, the attending medical physician-on-call, said to the medical chief resident and the first junior medical attending. "What seems to be the problem here?"

"Well," the chief resident explained, "This patient has been having a seizure."

"I see. Alright, get me up to speed on the situation with our patient, Demetrius Moutsiakis. What's the current situation?"

"This is the situation with Mr. Moot-see-cass."

The medical chief resident then gave Dr. Weinstein the abbreviated version of my story:

"Around three o'clock in the afternoon, a licensed practical nurse found our patient on the floor in his room having a seizure. The licensed practical nurse immediately went to the head nurse. The licensed practical nurse then paged the medical team to this floor, while the head nurse attended to the patient." The medical chief resident omitted the little adventure with the pediatric chief resident. "The junior medical residents and I assessed the situation. One of the junior medical residents paged you while the other junior medical resident and I tried to control the patient's seizures with valium. That was when you came in."

"I see. Thanks for the update," Dr. Weinstein replied.

Dr. Weinstein pondered his options in his head for a moment.

"Has anybody taken the patient to the radiology suite to have a CAT scan taken of his head?" he asked.

"Not yet," the medical chief resident replied. "Up to now, the patient had been seizing uncontrollably. The patient just now stopped seizing... no more than a few minutes ago, perhaps."

"Well, then, here's what I want you to do," Dr. Weinstein replied. "I want you to take the patient to radiology on the first floor, and have the patient get a CAT scan of the head without contrast. Maybe this way we can get a better look at what has been going on with our patient.

Once we get a better look at what is going on inside his head with the CAT scan, then we can decide where to go from here."

"Sounds good to me," the medical chief resident said to Dr. Weinstein.

"Alright, I'm going to downstairs to grab a bite to eat. Page me once you find out something from radiology."

Dr. Weinstein then went down the hall and out of view.

The medical chief resident then turned to address the two junior residents.

"We've got a lot to do," the medical chief resident began. "First, I need one of you to get me a stretcher and a gurney to move this patient around in. Can one of you get me a stretcher and a gurney?"

"I'll get them," said the second junior medical resident, who was happy to once again be doing something constructive.

"Great," the medical chief resident replied. With that, the second junior medical resident was off in search of a stretcher and gurney to take me from the pediatric ward on the third floor to the radiology suite on the first floor.

In the meantime, the medical chief resident and the first junior medical resident then turned to examine my lifeless body a little more carefully. I was not dead. I was still breathing. The valium had exhibited its desired effects. I was no longer having a seizure. As the two of them began to examine me more carefully, the second junior resident returned with a stretcher and gurney as promised.

"Here are the stretcher and a gurney," the second junior medical resident said to the medical chief resident, "As promised!'"

"Alright, then," the medical chief resident said, "I need the two of you to help me lift this patient first onto the gurney, and then onto the stretcher...all while causing as little trauma to the patient here as possible. This is what I need you two to do."

"One of you will stay by the patient's shoulders while the other one will stay by the patient's legs. The one by the patient's shoulders will make sure that the patient's head doesn't flop around, but stays straight. I will take the board and place the board alongside the patient. I will then stay by the patient's midsection. On the count of three, we will all lift the patient onto the gurney. Once the patient is atop the gurney, we will lift both the patient and the gurney onto the stretcher, and then secure the patient on the stretcher. After we secure the patient and the gurney on the stretcher, I will take the patient on the elevator down to the radiology suite located on the first floor. You two can come if you want to. It's up to you."

Both junior medical residents indicated that they wanted to join the medical chief resident to the radiology suite.

"Alright, then," the medical chief resident said, "We have a plan. Let's get this patient down to radiology."

With that, the three medical residents executed their plan without a single hitch. Within a matter of minutes, I was once again safely strapped into a gurney on a stretcher. It was almost like déjà vu all over again. There were several important differences, though, between this time and the last.

The last time I was strapped into a stretcher...during the ambulance ride from Bethpage parkway to Mid-Island Hospital in Bethpage...I was fully alert and oriented to my surroundings. I knew everything that was going on around me. This time, I was already well along my inevitable procession to a coma...a procession from which I had no personal recollection of at all.

Within about ten minutes, I had bid my final farewell to pediatrics in favor of the colder climate of the radiology suite on the first floor.

I am not simply taking poetic license here. All of the equipment…the X-rays, the CAT scan…had to be kept in a cool environment to prevent their becoming overheated. The radiology suite was truly quite cold.

In the radiology suite, the medical team was greeted by the receptionist. The medical chief resident spoke to the receptionist:

"Hello," the medical chief resident said, "My name is Dr. Kapoor. I am the medical chief resident for team B."

The medical chief resident pointed to his identification badge… hanging off the lower left pocket of his lab coat.

"Hi," the radiology receptionist replied, "I'm Paul, the receptionist for the radiology department. How can I help you?"

"My attending physician, Dr. Weinstein, asked me to take this patient, Mr. Moo-stick-ee-as, to radiology to have a CAT scan of the skull taken without contrast."

Dr. Kapoor continued: "We suspect that the patient may have had an acute bleed inside his skull, and we need to know where. That's why Dr. Weinstein ordered the CAT scan. The patient's situation is critical. If you have any questions, then you can take them up with my attending, Dr. Weinstein. If not, then I recommend that you hurry up and take that CAT scan as quickly as possible so that we can see exactly what is wrong with our patient."

"Very well," the radiology receptionist replied, "Just wait here a minute so that I can get a radiology technician to come and assist you. I'll be right back."

The radiology receptionist left his desk briefly, went somewhere behind the office out of sight, and then returned a short time later to the radiology front desk with what presumably was a radiology technician. The radiology receptionist faced the medical chief resident.

"This is Juan," the receptionist said. "He is one of our radiology technicians. He will assist you with the CT scan. If you at any point in time have questions regarding the performance of the CT scan, just ask Juan. He should be able to help. If he can't help, then he should at least be able to direct you to a person who can help you."

"Great," the medical chief resident replied. The medical chief resident then turned to Juan:

"Hello, Juan. My name is Dr. Kapoor. I'm the chief resident for Medical Team B. What we've got here is a very sick patient who needs a CAT scan of the skull without contrast right away so that we can see what exactly is wrong with him."

"Let's not waste any time, then," Juan replied. "Let's take this patient for his CAT scan of the skull."

With those words, Juan, the radiology technician, Dr. Kapoor, the medical chief resident and the rest of his entourage of residents marched me, the patient, still strapped to my gurney atop the stretcher, to the room where I was to have my CT scan.

I suppose that, had anybody been inclined to run an electroencephalogram (EEG) on me at that time in order to learn if I were still alive or dead, then that person would have discovered that, despite the valium-induced coma, I was not dead at all. Rather, that person would have learned that I was actually still alive, and screaming what I thought was a final, silent farewell to all.

I doubt that doing an EEG at that point would have made much of a difference regarding my medical care. Rather, doing an EEG now would have been a needless waste of time better spent attending to the cause of my seizure. Do I think that any knowledge gained by my EEG would or should have altered my treatment in any way? No, I do not... and that is my point.

Suffice it to say that, for now at least, I finally had my first of what would become several CT scans. After the radiology technician finished taking pictures of my brain and head, the radiology technician then went off somewhere in the bowels of the radiology department to develop the CT scan and present the images to the radiology resident on-call for urgent evaluation.

In the meantime, the medical chief resident and the rest of the entourage helped carry my seemingly lifeless body off of the CT scanner, and back onto the gurney, which was still lying atop the stretcher. Once I was securely fastened on the gurney atop the stretcher, the entire crew then proceeded to march me back to the lobby of the radiology suite.

The second junior medical resident was given the unenviable task of watching over my seemingly lifeless body in the lobby of the radiology suite, while the rest of the entourage returned to the general medical ward.

In the meantime, somewhere in the bowels of the radiology department, several CAT scans and plain X-ray films had been developed, and were being presented for "wet" read. The radiology resident on call had just returned from a rather unappetizing supper, and had the unenviable task of reading all the X-rays and CAT scans taken in the last few hours. The radiology resident sat back in his oversized, patented leather swivel chair, and began to review the films.

The report on the first X-ray asked to rule out fracture of the right radius and/or ulna…the two bones of the forearm. The radiology resident leaned forward to examine the X-ray more closely. The film was over-penetrated.

"This X-ray is over-penetrated, too, just like all the others I've seen today," the radiology resident muttered. "That's the sixth one that's over-penetrated. I think I should mention this to the attending. Maybe he can talk to the technicians to see if they can't fix the problem. This really ought to be fixed."

The radiology resident examined the film some more. There was no problem with the right radius at the elbow. The ulna also looked fine at the elbow. As the resident continued his examination, he could find nothing wrong with the film. All the epiphyses had been fused. This was obviously an X-ray from an adult.

"Alright," the radiology resident decided, "This film looks negative. No sign of fracture or dislocation of the right radius or ulna."

The radiology resident wrote a few notes in his pad next to the tray of X-rays and CAT scans.

"Next!" the radiology resident beamed.

The radiology pressed some buttons. The first film was magically whisked back into the tray, and a second film emerged. The radiology resident read the little blurb next to the film.

"Chest X-ray…adult…rule out pneumonia."

The radiology resident again moved closer to get a better view of the film. Like the prior film, this, too, was over-penetrated.

"Note to attending," the radiology resident said while writing on his pad, "Do something about the over-penetration problem."

The radiology resident then examined the film more carefully. White marks across the chest indicated where cardiovascular surgeons had operated in the past…probably a coronary artery bypass graft. There was a question of some possible enlargement of the thoracic aorta, but no frank aneurysm or coarctation. There were no indications of lobar pneumonia. Emphysema could not be ruled out due to over-penetration of this film.

The radiology continued with his notes as he spoke to himself:

"Prior coronary artery bypass graft evident. Dilation of thoracic aorta possible. Cannot exclude emphysema. No evidence of lobar pneumonia."

The radiology finished his note-taking and turned to the magic screen once again.

"Next!" he said as he pressed the button.

The second film was whisked away, and the third one stood in its stead. The radiology resident turned to read the blurb on the third film now facing him.

"CAT scan of the head without contrast."

The radiology moved in closer to get a better view. If these CAT films were also over-penetrated, the radiology resident didn't seem to notice.

The CAT scan was taken without contrast. None was necessary. On the left side of my head, a large white blob…a bleed…was occupying almost all the space inside the left side of my skull. The CT scan revealed a large mass of blood trapped just inside the left side of the skull…in the epidural space between the dura mater surrounding my brain on the inside and the skull on the outside. The large mass of blood was pushing down on the left side of my brain and actually squeezing its contents against the right side of my skull.

The picture presented here was a classic picture of a left epidural hematoma that a person sees on CT scan of the head. That was the type of picture that the radiology resident was now being presented with. The high-pressure, arterial blood from the ruptured left middle meningeal artery was flooding the virtual epidural space between the dura mater on the inside and the skull on the outside. This high-pressure, arterial bleed was threatening to squeeze my brain to death unless measures could be taken to relieve my brain of the pressure…and to relieve the pressure quickly.

The radiology resident quickly grasped the significance of my situation. Very few things in the life of a radiology resident could be considered life-or-death emergencies. This was such an emergency. Rather than simply have the radiology resident wait for the CT scan report to come up on the hospital's rudimentary computer network the next day, the radiology resident took the unusual step of calling the medical chief resident directly to report what the radiology resident had found.

Upon calling the medical chief resident, the radiology resident first cautioned the medical chief resident that the findings that were about to be shared with the medical chief resident were preliminary, and would have to be verified at some point by the radiology attending. The regular radiology attending for the day had gone home about one half an hour ago…around 4:30 PM. The radiology attending on-call had been paged. The radiology resident was awaiting a reply from his attending.

The radiology resident then presented his findings…regarding my CT scan…to the medical chief resident.

"Basically," the radiology resident reported, "The patient has a large left epidural hematoma, caused by a high-pressure, arterial bleed, most likely from the middle meningeal artery. This bleed was causing the contents of my brain to be crushed against the right side of the skull. Unless something is done…and done quickly…to remedy the situation and relieve the pressure in the patient's skull skull caused by this high-pressure, arterial bleed, then this patient will soon become another statistic."

"So what you're telling me," the medical chief resident said, "Is that the patient has a left epidural hematoma and, unless something can be done to relieve the pressure and stop the hemorrhaging, the patient will be dead?"

"That's it!"

"OK, thanks! I'll let my attending know right away. Thanks for all of your help."

"No problem."

With that, the medical chief resident hung up the phone.

The medical chief resident then paged Dr. Weinstein. When Dr. Weinstein failed to respond immediately to the page, the medical chief resident then tracked down Dr. Weinstein, who was having a not-so-quick bite to eat in the hospital cafeteria.

The medical chief resident gave Dr. Weinstein the abbreviated version of the radiology resident's report. The medical chief resident told Dr. Weinstein about the left epidural hematoma and the crushing of the patient's right side of the brain against the skull. The medical chief resident also re-iterated the radiology resident's admonishment for urgent action to avert a medical disaster.

What had originally been a simple case of a bicyclist falling off his bicycle and bumping his head quickly became more than this quiet community hospital could handle. A simple bump on the left side of the head had transformed itself into a massive left epidural hematoma that threatened to crush my brains against my right skull.

The medical attending, Dr. Weinstein, pondered the situation for only a moment.

"Alright," said Dr. Weinstein, "We need help, and we need it now. Here's what we are going to do."

Dr. Weinstein then elaborated his plan to the medical chief resident:

"We've got to contact neurosurgery. Who is the neurosurgeon-on-call? Dr. Nicolletti?"

Dr. Weinstein did not wait for a reply.

"Just page the neurosurgery service," Dr. Weinstein continued. "They should have the number in the medical nursing station on the second floor. Page them to my cell phone. When neurosurgery calls me back, I'll see what we can do to speed things up while they get themselves ready for surgery. You've got my cell number, I assume."

"Yes," Dr. Kapoor replied.

"Very well, then…let's get cracking!"

The medical chief resident, Dr. Kapoor, then went off to page the neurosurgery service. A plan had finally come together. All that was lacking was its execution.

CHAPTER NINE

Down, down, down went the trolley
Racing ever deeper down the track
Taking me to hell I had been certain,
While still hoping it would also take me back…

The date was still Thursday, 14 August 1991. The time was now roughly six o'clock in the evening. The place was my parents' house in Lindenhurst, about fifteen minutes southeast of Mid-Island Hospital.

Earlier that afternoon…around four-thirty in the afternoon…as a courtesy to the members of Medical Team B…the pediatric head nurse called my mom at her home. Alas, my mom was not home at that time. My mom was rarely at home at that time on any given Saturday afternoon. Instead, my mom would be exercising at the local Bally's Total Fitness Center, formerly known as Jack La Lane. This Saturday was no exception. After having gone to two different hospitals to see me and my dad, my mom went to Jack La Lane to exercise…trying mighty hard to cope with the thought of both of the men in her life… her husband and now her son…in different hospitals.

Unable to speak to my mom directly, the pediatric head nurse left my mom a message on the answering machine:

"Hello, my name is Mrs. Bellweather. I am the Pediatric Head Nurse at Mid-Island Hospital. I am calling in regards to a patient in the medical service...a Mr. Demetrius Moutsiakis. Your son has experienced some unforeseen complications. I wanted to ask if you could return to Mid-Island Hospital as soon as possible. When you return to Mid-Island Hospital, just come to the front lobby and speak to the receptionist. Tell the receptionist that you are Demetrius' mom... your son was involved in a bicycle accident. Somebody will come down to help you as soon as possible. Again, if you have any questions, call me. My name is Mrs. Bellweather. I am the pediatric head nurse."

The pediatric head nurse then hung up the phone, and resumed her more normal duties.

Shortly before six o'clock, my mom returned from Bally's Total Fitness Center to discover that the answering machine in the living room was flashing. Somebody called the house while my mom was at the gym. My mom quickly removed her gym clothes, towel and bathing suit from the gym bag, dropped her gym bag on the floor, hung her gym clothes, towel and bathing suit outside on the clothes line to dry, and then turned her attention to the answering machine.

Upon pressing the red "PLAY" button, the answering machine responded in its usual, cheery, synthetic voice:

"Hello. You have one message." The machine paused temporarily, and then resumed its message. "First message..."

The voice now heard on the answering machine was a female voice... that of the pediatric head nurse. The answering machine continued:

"Hello, my name is Mrs. Bellweather. I am the Pediatric Head Nurse at Mid-Island Hospital. I am calling in regards to a patient in the medical service...a Mr. Demetrius Moutsiakis."

My mother nearly dropped the phone right then and there. My mom's hands began trembling uncontrollably.

The voice of the pediatric head nurse continued: "Your son has experienced some unforeseen complications. I wanted to ask if you could return to Mid-Island Hospital as soon as possible. When you return to Mid-Island Hospital, just come to the front lobby and speak to the receptionist. Tell the receptionist that you are Demetrius' mom… your son was involved in a bicycle accident. Somebody will come down to help you as soon as possible."

My mom could hardly believe what she was hearing. She was becoming downright frantic.

"Again, if you have any questions, call me. My name is Mrs. Bellweather. I am the pediatric head nurse." The pediatric head nurse then finished the message and hung up.

The answering machine then returned to its perpetually cheery, synthetic voice, and continued: "End of messages. No new messages…"

By that point, my mom wasn't listening any longer. My mom didn't care what else the answering machine had to say. The answering machine had said enough. The answering machine had said that her son was experiencing unforeseen complications, and that my mom needed to come to Mid-Island Hospital. The answering machine had said enough.

When my father was first hospitalized in Syosset…while I was vacationing to Europe…my mom had spoken to our back-door neighbor, Mike, about what had happened to father. Mike had re-assured my mom that, if anything like this were to happen again, he would be able to take my mom to the hospital. My mom intended to take Mike at his word.

My mom first looked out the kitchen window in the back of the house to see if Mike's car...a silver-and-black sport utility vehicle...was in the driveway. It was. She next looked across the yard to see if Mike was in the house or yard. She wasn't sure. Unsure where Mike might be, she then walked back to the living room, picked up the phone, and called Mike on the phone.

Somebody picked up on the other end. "Hello," that person said. "This is Mike Zampella."

"Hi, Mike, this is Ann, your neighbor from across the yard" my mom replied.

"Hi, Ann! What's up?"

"Remember what you said to me before about taking me and Leon to the hospital if Leon got sick?"

"I remember. I thought Leon was already in the hospital, though."

"It's not Leon. This time it's Meme. He's in Mid-Island Hospital in Bethpage. He was in a bicycle accident. A nurse from Mid-Island just called, and said he is having some sort of complications. They asked me to come in. I'd go by myself...except I feel that if I do go by myself, I'll get into an accident. Then we'll all be in the hospital."

"No...I know what you mean. Do you want me to take you to Mid-Island Hospital?"

"Could you?"

"Sure! I think I know where Mid-Island Hospital is. It's off the Seaford-Oyster Bay Expressway. I can be over in front of your house in five minutes."

"Great! I'll fill you in on what I know so far on the way to Mid-Island. Alright, then. Bye!"

My mom hung up the phone. She quickly grabbed her things, left the house, and locked the front door. Mike drove up from around the corner, and stopped by the front gate. He opened the passenger-side door of the car.

"Quick…get in!" Mike urged.

My mom climbed into the passenger-side door of the sport utility vehicle. She sat in the passenger seat, and fastened her seatbelt.

"I know where Mid-Island is," Mike began. "Just tell me what happened to Meme, and why he's in the hospital."

"OK. I'll talk. You drive," my mom replied.

My mom explained the circumstances surrounding my accident to Mike as Mike drove them to Mid-Island Hospital. Within fifteen minutes, Mike was dropping my mom off at the lobby of Mid-Island Hospital and parking the car. Mike was a little faster at driving than my mom. What can I say? Mike was a policeman for New York City.

My mom entered the lobby of Mid-Island, and approached the receptionist at the front desk.

"Excuse me," my mom began, "My name is Ann. I just received a call from Mrs. Bellweather, the pediatric head nurse, asking me to return to the hospital on account of some unforeseen complications about my son, Demetrius. I'm his mother. Could you tell me what kind of complications we are talking about?"

"I'm sorry. Could I have your full name?" the receptionist asked.

"I'm sorry. My name is Ann Moutsiakis. I'm Demetrius' mother."

"Thank you. Just give me a minute so that I can look your name up on the computer."

The receptionist then turned her attention briefly to the computer monitor and keyboard situated in front of her. After typing something on the keyboard, and then pressing the enter key a few times, the receptionist turned her attention back to my mom.

"OK, Mrs. Moutsiakis. I have your son's name on my computer," the receptionist said.

The receptionist suddenly remembered something.

"Wait a minute," the receptionist continued. "Somebody wanted me to do something."

The receptionist turned her attention briefly to a hand-written note scribbled on a Post-it note just to the right of computer monitor. She then turned her attention back to my mom.

The receptionist continued: "I have a note here from Dr. Kapoor, the chief resident for Medicine Team B. I'm not sure what the exact situation is. I spoke briefly to the medical chief resident. He told me to look for you. When I see you, I was supposed to contact him...Dr. Kapoor...on his pager. I've got the number here somewhere."

The receptionist then began fumbling through a small pile of her papers.

"Just give me a minute," the receptionist continued, while still searching for the lost paper.

"Aha!" the receptionist exclaimed. "I've found it"

The receptionist then pulled out a paper with a list of names and pager numbers on it. The receptionist scrolled down the list until she found the proper name.

"Here it is," the receptionist said. "I'm to page Dr. Kapoor when you come in. I'll page Dr. Kapoor right away."

The receptionist then paged Dr. Kapoor to the number for the front desk.

"I just paged Dr. Kapoor to this number. He should get back to me shortly," the receptionist said.

"Thanks," replied my mom.

"In the meantime, if you want, you can have a seat anywhere you like. There are plenty of open seats."

"No thanks. I think I'll just stand for now."

"Suit yourself."

While waiting for word from Dr. Kapoor, Mike came in from the parking lot. Mike saw my mom standing by the reception desk.

"Ann!" Mike called out.

"Hi! I just spoke to the receptionist," my mom replied. "She paged the chief resident. He should be coming down shortly to speak to me."

"Good. How are you holding up?"

"I've had better days!"

"Haven't we all?"

Within a few minutes, the receptionist's phone rang. The receptionist picked up the phone, and spoke briefly with the person on the other end. The receptionist then hung up the phone, and turned once again to face my mom, who was waiting anxiously by the receptionist's window.

"That was Dr. Kapoor. He will be coming down to speak with you shortly," the receptionist said."

"Thanks again," my mom said. "By the way, this is my neighbor, Mike. I think I'll take you up on your previous offer now. We'll grab some chairs over here, and sit down until Dr. Kapoor comes to talk to us."

"Sounds fine with me…"

My mom spotted two large, comfortable, unoccupied chairs on the far side of the lobby. Mike and my mom walked over to the chairs, and sat down. As Mike and my mom talked about the possible nature of these unforeseen complications, memories flooded my mom's mind. My mom shared some of these recollections of me with Mike.

My mom hearkened back to the first time the five of us moved to my parents' house in Greece in 1972. My mom was reminded of a picture that my father had taken of me…then only three years old… romping through the fields of what must have seemed to me to be the high chaparral at the time. Thinking of this picture brought tears to my mom's eyes. I had always been such a happy child.

My mom also told Mike how proud she had been when she saw me crossing the finish line at the Long Island Half-Marathon in Jones Beach State Park back when I was still in high school. My mom also told him how much fun she had seeing me as a young Patrick Dennis in the high school musical production of <u>Mame</u>.

As my mom sat with Mike in the lobby of Mid-Island Hospital, recalling memories of better days with her son, a somewhat shorter, Indian or Pakistani gentleman of about thirty years of age approached her, and said:

"Hello," in his soft-spoken, Indian accent, "My name is Dr. Kapoor.

I am chief resident for the medical team taking care of Demetrius. Are you his mother?"

The sound of Dr. Kapoor's voice interrupted my mom's recollections of her son.

"Why, yes," my mom replied. "My name is Ann Moutsiakis. I am Demetrius' mother. Are you his doctor? What news can you tell me about my son? Is he OK? Where is he? Can I see him now?"

I was not the only recipient of my mom's barrage of questions. My mom was an equal opportunity interrogator.

Taken temporarily aback by my mom's barrage of questions, Dr. Kapoor paused to collect his thoughts. He then proceeded to answer her questions as best he could.

"I am the chief medical resident. I am part of the team assigned to your son's case. Apparently, the fall off the bicycle that your son had experienced proved to be a little more serious than originally anticipated." Dr. Kapoor said.

"Your son had a seizure while in the pediatric ward," Dr. Kapoor continued. "He has been taken from the pediatric ward to radiology to have a CAT scan. We believe that your son may have had a bleed inside his skull. We are hoping that the CAT scan will tell us where exactly the bleeding is taking place."

Dr. Kapoor paused briefly to collect himself again, and then continued: "I want to ask you, does your son have any prior history of seizures or epilepsy?"

"What...seizures?" my mom replied...a little taken aback by the question. "I don't think so...not as far as I know. No, my son has no history of seizures. In fact, this is the first time that my son was ever admitted to a hospital for any reason."

"Your son has no prior history of seizures or epilepsy, then. That is an important consideration. It suggests that epilepsy, a history of recurring seizures, is likely not a factor in your son's case."

"No...if my son had a history of seizures, I think I would have known about it. Nope...no seizures..."

"That's good to know. As I said before, your son is currently having a CAT scan in radiology. When your son finishes in radiology, you will be able to see him. I must warn you beforehand, however, that your son will probably not be able to speak with you. Your son had a seizure. I was able to control the seizure, but only with rather heavy medication. Chances are that he will still be unconscious when he returns from radiology. When your son is finished in radiology, I will make sure you can see him. That is where things stand for now. If there are any changes, I will keep you abreast of things."

"Thank you very much. I would really appreciate that."

Dr. Kapoor then took his leave of my mom in order to better attend to the matter at hand...in this case, me.

Mike and my mom then resumed their previous recollections.

While Mike and my mom continued their conversation, Dr. Kapoor would have his conversations with the radiology resident first, and then with Dr. Weinstein. Dr. Kapoor would page the neurology service to Dr. Weinstein's cell phone number so that Dr. Weinstein could reply directly to the page.

Sometime between seven and eight o'clock in the evening, while Mike and my mom were pondering the possibilities before them... Dr. Kapoor reappeared in the lobby with a gurney atop a stretcher. Dr. Kapoor approached my mom, and said to her in his accent that still sounded either Indian or Pakistani:

"Mrs. Moutsiakis, I have brought your son back from radiology…"

Dr. Kapoor was still speaking, but at this point, it didn't matter. My mom had tuned Dr. Kapoor out completely. My mom was focused instead on her son lying on a gurney atop a stretcher.

My mom was overcome by the scene before her. "Meme," my mom cried out to me. "Oh, Meme…"

My mom cried out for her son, Meme, but her son did not respond. Words could not describe the deep, dark despair that engulfed my mom. Shock, anger, hurt and despair hit her all at once. For once, she was speechless.

Meme was the nickname that my parents gave me when I was really small. Meme is also a nickname with its roots as ancient as Greece itself. There is a truly inspiring and perhaps, one might even say, uplifting story behind the nickname. Perhaps I will share this story with you at a later date. That will have to wait for now, though.

Sensing that my mom was no longer listening to Dr. Kapoor, Dr. Kapoor thought it best to stay silent until my mom could collect herself.

Eventually, my mom re-emerged from her trance-like state above my withered body, and turned to face Dr. Kapoor again.

"So what can you tell me about my son?" my mom asked.

"Well," Dr. Kapoor replied, "Your son has what is called a left epidural hematoma…that means it is on the left side of his head. An epidural hematoma is a bleed on the inside of a person's skull that is usually caused by direct trauma, although it can be caused by other reasons."

"OK."

"In an epidural hematoma, a blood vessel feeding the brain bursts. Blood rushes inside the skull until it has no place to go. Once the blood has no place to go, the pressure starts to build up. Unless a way can be found for the pressure inside the skull to be relieved, the pressure inside your son's skull will end up crushing your son's brain, and he will die."

"I see. Unless something is done, my son will die. How do you plan to release the pressure inside my son's skull?"

"I personally can't do anything. That is the sad reality of the situation. However, neurosurgery can do something. The neurosurgery team has been contacted. As we speak, the neurosurgical team is being assembled in this hospital so that these neurosurgeons can open up your skull to relieve some of the pressure on your son's brain."

Dr. Kapoor pointed to his own left temporal region and his left temple in order to provide visualization for my mom.

Dr. Kapoor then continued: "Once the skull is cut open, and the artery is fixed, the pressure inside your son's skull will be released. Once the pressure has been released, we will have to wait and see how much function remains. At this point, we do not know. Your son may be fine. Your son may never wake up again. We won't know right away. We will have to wait to see."

"Thank you," my mom replied. "I truly appreciate everything you have done on my son's behalf. Again, I thank you."

Before turning once again to leave, Dr. Kapoor spoke once more to my mom, who was no longer sitting by this point, but rather was now standing upright beside my withered body on the gurney atop the stretcher.

"The neurosurgical team is almost ready. Until the neurosurgical team arrives to take your son to surgery, you may stay in the lobby to look after your son. I don't see a reason not to."

"That would be great," my mom replied.

"I will leave you for now. As I said before, someone will come shortly to take your son to surgery."

"Don't worry. When the time comes, I will let him go."

Dr. Kapoor then returned to the same place where he came from. That left just me on the gurney atop a stretcher, my mom by my side, and Mike next to her.

Mike softly muttered words of encouragement to my mom as I lay unconscious atop the gurney. My mom tried with all her might to will me to get better.

Suddenly, a thought crossed my mom's mind.

"We have to call our priest!" my mom exclaimed. "I have to talk to the front desk."

My mom approached the receptionist, and said:

"Excuse me. Can I use a phone? I have to call my priest so that he can do last rites on my son."

"Sure," the receptionist replied. "You can use this phone over here."

The receptionist pointed to the adjoining window, which was unoccupied at the moment.

"Thanks!"

My mom went to the adjoining window, and set her purse down.

She scrambled around her purse until she found her pocket address book. She searched the address book for St. Nicholas, the name of our church. She found the number for our priest, and called it:

"Hello, this is Father Max," our local Greek Orthodox priest for Babylon, Father Max, replied.

"Hi, Father Max, this is Ann," my mom replied.

"How are you and Leon? Is something wrong with Leon again?"

"No, it's not Leon this time. It's Demetrius. He's in Mid-Island Hospital. I need you to perform last rites on him."

"On Demetrius?"

"Yes, on Demetrius! He's at Mid-Island Hospital. He's had a seizure. He has a left epidural hematoma. They are getting him ready for emergency surgery to relieve the pressure in his skull. I need you to come to Mid-Island to perform last rites on him before he goes under the knife."

"Oh, come on! It can't be that serious. I'll tell you what. Why don't I just stop by tomorrow to see Demetrius? You said he's in Mid-Island hospital, right?"

"You can stop by tomorrow, but my son may not be there tomorrow." My mom was furious! Father Max was our priest. That was what priests were supposed to do…perform last rites! What's wrong with him?

"If anything happens," my mom continued, "It's on your hands." My mom then slammed the receiver down on the phone. After first regaining her composure, my mom turned back to the receptionist.

"Is there a Catholic priest here who can perform last rites on my son?" my mom asked.

"Yes," the receptionist replied, "There is always one on standby. Would you like me to call him?"

"If you could…"

"I'll send him here right away."

"Thanks!"

My mom then turned back to Mike while the receptionist called for the local priest on call.

"I called for a Catholic priest to perform last rites on Meme," she told Mike.

Within a short time, the priest came, and performed last rites on me. Last rites may be performed on the dying, but they are actually for those who are left behind.

In due time, somebody approached my mom from somewhere down one of the corridors that would soon become sickeningly familiar. He introduced himself as a member of the neurosurgical team.

"Hello," the neurosurgical team member began, "My name is…"

The member of the neurosurgical team said his name, but my mom was not listening. In fact, my mom was just barely clinging onto her tenuous grasp with reality. Her husband was already in the HIP medical center in Syosset…for the second time in about two months. Now, to top it off, her son was in a second hospital…about five minutes away from my father…where neurosurgeons were taking him so that they could drill holes in the left side of his skull, and pray for a miracle.

Hopefully, my mom thought, her son would survive the surgery and its oft-neglected aftermath. There were never any guarantees when it came to surgery. Even if her son did manage to survive the surgery, there was no way of knowing what condition her son would end up in after the surgery. Would he recover completely from his bicycle accident? Would he remain in a coma forever…like Karen Ann Quinlan…adrift in parts unknown?

"Only time will tell," the chief medical resident had said to my mom. "Only time will tell."

My mom was the only one in the house. Both her parents had died over a decade ago in California. Both had suffered the ill effects of that sinister habit called smoking. In the meantime, my dad was in a nearby hospital recovering from <u>Revenge of the Gall Bladder</u>. My mom's older son, George, was still in Detroit, MI…finishing work for his Ph.D. in Psychology. My mom's daughter, Vaia, was still in Melbourne, FL… earning her Master's degree in Education so that she could continue teaching. Now I was lying literally on death's doorstep.

My mom was the only one in the house.

The neurosurgeon and my mom exchanged pleasantries for a brief moment. The neurosurgeon discussed with my mom what the neurosurgery team intended to do with me.

My mom didn't care what the neurosurgeon had to say. My mom's mind was numb with grief. The neurosurgeon continued anyway, oblivious to my mom's apparent lack of interest.

"First, your son will be anesthetized. After the anesthesia kicks in, and your son is anesthetized…"

My mom wasn't paying this man any mind. The neurosurgeon's words flew in one ear and out the other.

At last the neurosurgeon finished speaking. My mom was still focused on me. Finally, my mom managed to break free of the spell cast by my helpless frame, and faced the neurologist directly.

"If you don't have any more questions," the neurosurgical team member said, "Then I will take your son to surgery right away."

"Just one thing," my mom replied before leaving me in the hands of the neurosurgical team, "Fight, Meme, fight! You can do it. Fight!"

My mom released then her son into the custody of the neurosurgeons. My mom watched as the neurosurgeon carried me, on the gurney atop my stretcher, across the lobby, down a different hallway, and out of sight.

CHAPTER TEN

To the person that had said:
"The road to Hell is paved with good intentions."
I would counter simply here:
"And who said it was paved?"

Somewhere in the deep, dark caverns of my mind, I sensed a certain inner turmoil as I reached the gates of Hell. As my brain lay crushed against the right side of my skull…like a child trapped in a cyclotron that simply refused to stop spinning…I thought that surely I must have fallen as far down as possible. There was simply no way here that I could sink down any further.

I was wrong. I was, as usual, being overly optimistic. I had not quite reached the gates of Hell. I had not yet reached rock bottom. I had at least one more flight of stairs to fall down before I could say that I reached rock bottom. The worst was yet to come.

My dear friends back in neurosurgery were to make certain of that fact. I still had one more flight of stairs to fall down.

My mom watched from her position on the far side of the lobby at

Mid-Island Hospital as the neurosurgeon wheeled me on the gurney atop my stretcher down the corridor and toward the distant operating room. As the neurosurgeon pressed onward, the neurosurgeon was soon joined by the other members of the team. The entire team of physicians and technicians was off to rescue me from certain death… so they thought.

The neurosurgical team made its way down the corridor toward the distant operating room. Mike and my mom stayed back in the hospital lobby…waiting and praying that God would not fail us in our time of need.

While the neurosurgeons and most of the ancillary crew were busy preparing for the upcoming surgery in the manner in which they saw fit, the anesthesiologist and his own technician were already in the operating arena…armed with their intravenous-fluid bags and their sedating medications…preparing for what was supposed to be…from their point of view…yet another routine operation.

The chief neurosurgeon made a brief appearance in the operating arena for one final pre-operative assessment before exiting to the prep room in order to scrub up for the upcoming surgery. The neurosurgical fellows followed the chief neurosurgeon like lost puppy dogs…trying to make them appear as useful as possible while staying out of the way once their usefulness had ended. They, too, exited to the prep room in order to scrub up for the surgery. Finally, the neurosurgical nurses made their own brief appearances in the operating arena to attend to some last-minute nursing needs before exiting to the prep room in order to scrub up for the upcoming surgery. The entire surgical team was good to go, and ready to commence the surgical intervention.

The surgery commenced in the usual manner. Before the actual surgical cutting and releasing was to begin, the area of skin, hair, bruising, and debris around the left side of my head was first washed clean to minimize the risk of subsequent infection. Next, the portion of the head suspected by CT scan of being affected by the left epidural hematoma was shaved clean of any hair using a single-edged razor blade.

Finally, once the left front portion of my skull had been shaved clean, a surgical pencil was used to mark off the portion of the skull that was to be sliced open in order to identify the offending artery, fix it, and release the pressure inside the skull.

On one side of the surgical curtain…the side of the curtain where my head lay in helpless anticipation of the upcoming events…the neurosurgical team went about the business of relieving the pressure that was threatening to end my brief life as a future physician. On the other side…the side of the curtain where the rest of my body was supposed to be comfortably resting, the anesthesiologist and his assistant went about the mundane business of ensuring that the entire experience with the anesthetics and other drugs associated with the surgery was as uneventful as possible.

On one side, the neurosurgical team had at last completed its preliminary assessment of the situation, and started the process of cutting open the left side of my skull just above and in front of my left ear with a buzz-saw so that the appropriate artery could be found and fixed. On the other side, the anesthesiologist had already provided for me all the anesthetics and ancillary medications that would ensure that I was in a deep, dark slumber for the duration of the surgery. The anesthesiologist at last allowed himself to sit back in his chair next to his technician and relax.

Every five minutes, the anesthesiologist made sure that matters remained mundane. While attending to these mundane matters at hand, the anesthesiologist noticed something rather peculiar. On the other side of the curtain, the neurosurgeons were still busily attending to the matter of the surgical slice-and-dice that would relieve the pressure inside my skull. The neurosurgeons were oblivious of any anesthetic anomalies. On his own side of the surgical curtain, however, the anesthesiologist noticed something rather peculiar indeed. My core body temperature was rising.

The anesthesiologist couldn't quite pinpoint the exact time my body temperature began to rise. When the anesthesiologist had initially begun monitoring my vital sign as a routine part of surgical care, all of my vital signs had been in order. My temperature was 97 °F. My blood pressure was 106/68 mm Hg. My pulse was 60/minute. My respirations were 12/minute and regular. All of my vital signs were within the normal range at the time. Absolutely nothing was out of the ordinary.

When the anesthesiologist next checked my vital signs immediately following the administration of the anesthetics and ancillary medications, still nothing seemed too out of the ordinary. My temperature was hovering somewhere between 98.6 and 98.7 °F. All of the other vital signs were within normal limits. Again, nothing was out of the ordinary. This was still just another routine operation.

Now, however, when the anesthesiologist checked my vital signs again…perhaps ten or fifteen minutes after the administration of the anesthetics and ancillary medications…something did not seem quite right. My temperature was now 100.2 °F. My blood pressure was now 128/52 mm Hg. My pulse was 84/minute. My respirations were about15/minute. My temperature…while not yet high enough to be considered febrile…nevertheless was disturbing. Both my pulse and respiration rate were higher now than when the surgery commenced. In addition, my blood pressure appeared odd.

The first number in the blood pressure reading is called the systolic pressure…the peak pressure that one sees after the heart has just contracted. Normal systolic pressure is 120 mm Hg. Children and well-conditioned athletes typically have lower resting systolic pressure… between 90 and 110 mm Hg. My resting systolic pressure was 106 mm Hg.

The second number in the blood pressure reading is called the diastolic pressure…the lowest pressure that one sees before the heart contracts again. Normal diastolic pressure is 80 mm Hg. Again, children and well-conditioned athletes typically have lower resting diastolic pressure…between 60 and 80 mm Hg. My resting diastolic pressure was 68 mm Hg.

The difference between the systolic and diastolic pressures is called the pulse pressure. The pulse pressure is most useful when considered as a fraction of the systolic pressure. For example, the normal resting pulse pressure is (120 – 80 mm Hg)/120 mm Hg, or roughly one third. Even among well-trained athletes, the resting pulse pressure is roughly one third. Resting pulse pressure is relatively stable.

Certain things can cause the pulse pressure to rise. Aerobic exercises such as running, swimming, or cycling can cause the pulse pressure to rise. Fever due to any cause can also cause the pulse pressure to rise.

My current condition reminded the anesthesiologist of a medical/surgical condition that he first learned about during his residency training in anesthesiology. That condition was also associated with increased pulse pressure. That condition was called malignant hyperthermia.

Malignant hyperthermia is one of the banes of anesthesiologists' existence. Malignant hyperthermia has been responsible for an unusually large proportion of anesthetic complications and deaths over the course of the last seventy-five years. Malignant hyperthermia has been around since the invention of anesthesia.

Malignant hyperthermia is a condition that occurs sporadically...to a select few. People who have malignant hyperthermia are believed to have abnormal responses to certain general anesthetics. Local anesthetics...such as lidocaine or Novocain given to patients in a dental office...do not have the same response as general anesthetics. Only general anesthetics such as halothane...or muscle relaxants such as succinyl choline...appear capable of inducing hyperthermic reactions in susceptible individuals.

When susceptible individuals are given certain general anesthetics or muscle relaxants, several things happen...none of which are very nice.

First, as the anesthetic or muscle relaxant enters the body, the agent is dispersed throughout the body...to places such as the brain, bone, and muscle tissues. It is in muscle tissue that these adverse effects of the anesthetics become manifest.

Normally, there is very little calcium floating around freely in either the bloodstream or muscle tissue. Normally, the calcium found in muscle tissue is kept trapped in containers called sarcoplasmic reticuli.

When certain general anesthetics or muscle relaxants find their way inside the muscle tissue, that agent…for reasons that are not entirely clear…causes the sarcoplasmic reticulum to release large amounts of calcium into the cytoplasm of the muscle. The release of large amounts of calcium activates the muscle tissue. The activated muscle tissue begins to contract.

Now, when a single muscle fiber contracts, that muscle fiber produces a tiny burst of energy in the form of heat. When an entire muscle…such as, say, your biceps muscle on your arm or your quadriceps muscle on your thigh, that muscle produces a somewhat larger burst of energy in the form of heat.

Now imagine not simply one muscle fiber or one muscle contracting, but rather every single muscle in your body contracting at once. Furthermore, imagine now that this is not simply a one-time event, but instead imagine every muscle fiber contracting at a rate of three times per second for as long as the calcium is still in the cytoplasm. Now you can begin to realize how some general anesthetics or muscle relaxants…when given to susceptible persons…can result in a massive burst of energy in the form of heat.

This was the exact situation that was now happening to me.

My muscles were overheating, and my core body temperature was beginning to rise. The current medical condition that the anesthesiologist now faced bore an uncanny resemblance to the description of malignant hyperthermia that he had read about in his anesthesiology textbooks back in the beginning of his residency training.

Untreated, just about everybody with malignant hyperthermia… challenged with inappropriate anesthetics such as halothane or muscle relaxants such as succinyl choline…dies as a result. Essentially, everyone experiencing an episode of malignant hyperthermia…who does not receive prompt care…spontaneously combusts. Even with the appropriate treatment…which generally involves removal of the offending anesthetic or muscle relaxant and rapid cooling…far too many people with this condition die anyway.

I emphasize the term treatment over cure here. Treatment generally involves the amelioration or lessening of offensive symptoms. Cure implies total eradication or elimination of both an offending agent and its associated symptoms. Cure implies a return to baseline. Cure is an inappropriate term here.

The anesthesiologist had never seen a real case of malignant hyperthermia before. Up to now, he had only ever read about it in his anesthesiology textbooks. In fact, most standard medical and surgical textbooks either do not mention malignant hyperthermia at all, or offer only a cursory explanation of the term with little additional elaboration. The anesthesiologist suspected that was what he was witnessing now.

The anesthesiologist briefly left his post on the anesthesiologist's side of the surgical curtain to the hands of the anesthesiologist's assistant so that he could track down my mom, and speak to her.

The anesthesiologist left the surgical suite through the anesthesiologist's entrance/exit. The anesthesiologist hurriedly left the operating room area, and then proceeded rather briskly down the corridor past the elevators to the main lobby. The time at this point must have been between nine and ten o'clock in the evening. The anesthesiologist quickly spotted my mom sitting down in her chair in the lobby talking to another gentleman. The anesthesiologist approached my mom from across the lobby, and said:

"Excuse me, madam, but are you the mother of Demetrius?" the anesthesiologist asked.

The anesthesiologist didn't even attempt to pronounce my last name for fear of embarrassment at the thought of mispronouncing it…which the anesthesiologist probably would have done.

"Yes," my mom replied. "I am Mrs. Moutsiakis. I am Demetrius' mother. This is Mike, my neighbor. Is the surgery already over? Can I see my son now? How is he? Is he OK?"

Once again, my mom had commenced with the twenty questions. No one was immune to the twenty questions.

The anesthesiologist turned to face my mother directly.

"We haven't been properly introduced. My name is Dr. Leichtkopf. I am the anesthesiologist in charge of your son, Demetrius. The surgery is not yet over. The surgery is still taking place now."

"Then why do you want to speak with me?" my mom interjected.

My mom was concerned that something regarding the surgery was going terribly wrong. My mom was scared. After all, my mom had reasoned, why else would this anesthesiologist want to speak with me… unless something had gone terribly wrong?

My mom interjected again: "Is everything alright?"

"There may be a problem," Dr. Leichtkopf started.

Those were five words that my mom did not want to hear. Those were five words from a medical specialist that nobody wanted to hear.

"What do you mean?" my mom asked…almost afraid what the answer might be. "What type of problem are you talking about?"

"Just stay calm," Mike reassured Ann. "Everything will be fine."

My mom was doing her best to maintain her composure. She tried hard not to get hysterical. Hysterical outbursts were in nobody's best interests. Hysterical outbursts would only result in a third hospitalization in the family...this time in a psychiatric ward somewhere on Long Island.

"I want to ask you a question," Dr. Leichtkopf continued...still facing my mom directly. "Have you or anybody else in your family ever reported having a condition known as malignant hyperthermia?"

This question proved so far afield as to come from a completely different ballpark. Up to this point, my mom had very little medical training. I was the up-and-coming physician...not her.

"I'm sorry. What?" my mom asked.

My mom stood there...dumbfounded...like a deer in the headlights. My mom had no idea what this doctor was talking about, and made no attempt to hide that fact.

"I'm sorry. I owe you some sort of explanation first. You see," Dr. Leichtkopf continued, "There is a condition called malignant hyperthermia. In this condition, people who receive certain general anesthetics have bad reactions to these anesthetics. Some people even die."

"Now," Dr. Leichtkopf continued, "These bad reactions to anesthetics tend to run in families. That is why I am asking you if your son...or anybody else in your family...has ever had general anesthesia in the past?"

"What, are you kidding? My son...anesthetized? My son hadn't even been to the hospital until now. Oh, wait...my son did have Novocain when the dentist removed his wisdom teeth. Is that what you mean?"

"Actually, I don't mean local anesthetics. I mean specifically certain general anesthetics such as halothane or isofluorane."

"I am sure that my son has never had any general anesthetics in the past. Nobody in my family has had anesthesia."

"Nobody else in your or your father's family has had bad reactions to anesthetics in the past?"

"No, not that I am aware of..."

"OK. Nobody in your immediate family has had a bad reaction to anesthetics. What is your racial background? Are either you or your husband of American Indian or Alaskan Native heritage?"

"What? Did you say 'American Indian'?"

"Yes. Why?"

"Well, my husband is Greek, as you might have guessed from the last name, Moutsiakis. I, however, am not Greek, but American. In fact, I have Native American roots from both sides of my family."

"I see."

"I'll tell you what," my mom concluded, "I don't have any history of...how do you call it...malignant hyperthermia? I don't have any history of malignant hyperthermia in my family that I am aware of. I do have Native American roots from both sides of my family, however. Now you are telling me that I may have inherited this condition...this malignant hyperthermia...from one of my Native American ancestors. I'll tell you what. Just to be on the safe side, I'll just go ahead and assume that my son has malignant hyperthermia. That way, you can do whatever you have to do to make sure that my son survives this surgery. Does that sound alright with you?"

"Yes. That is fine."

"Any other questions?" my mom asked.

"No," the anesthesiologist replied. "That's all I needed to know. Thank you for all your help. I'd best get back to the surgery now. I left the anesthetic care for your son in the capable hands of my assistant. However, I'd better make sure everything is still OK."

"OK. I won't keep you, then. It was nice to meet you. Bye!"

With that, the anesthesiologist quickly turned around, left the lobby, hurried down the corridor toward the operating room, donned his face mask, and returned to the anesthesiology side of the surgical curtain. Perhaps five minutes had elapsed since the anesthesiologist left the anesthesiologist's side of the surgical curtain in order to speak with my mom.

When the anesthesiologist returned to my operating table, the situation had, in fact, changed...but not for the better.

When the anesthesiologist left the operating room to speak to my mom, my vital signs were the following:
Temperature: 100.2°F   (37.9°C)
Pulse: 84/min Respirations: 15/min Blood pressure: 128/52 mm Hg

When the anesthesiologist returned to the operating room after speaking to my mom, my vital signs were now the following:
Temperature: 102.8°F (39.3°C)
Pulse: 102/min Respirations: 18/min Blood pressure: 144/48 mm Hg

My vital signs were not improving. The vital signs were getting worse. My temperature was now 102.8 (39.3°C). I could now be considered as having a fever. My pulse was now racing at over one hundred beats per minute. In medical terms, I had tachycardia. At eighteen breaths per minute, I was also breathing faster as well. The medical term for that was tachypnea. My systolic pressure suggested hypertension, while my diastolic pressure suggested hypotension. My pulse pressure was now markedly elevated. All of my vital signs suggested that I was having an episode of malignant hyperthermia.

The anesthesiologist looked back briefly at the temperature monitor. The temperature reading was now 102.9°F (39.4°C).

"Have you looked at the patient's vital signs?" the anesthesiologist asked his assistant. "Have you seen them?"

"Yes," the anesthesiology assistant replied somewhat timidly. "It appears that the patient has a fever."

"Very good! The patient has a fever. Ten minutes ago, the patient did not have a fever. What is different about the patient now as compared to just ten minutes ago? Absolutely nothing! There is only one thing that can cause a rapid, sudden rise in temperature…us."

"What do you mean?"

"I just stepped out for a moment to speak to the patient's mother. I believe that the patient may be experiencing an episode of malignant hyperthermia. The patient is apparently having an adverse reaction to either one of the anesthetics or muscle relaxants we are giving him. If we do nothing, the patient will die…and we will have no one to blame but ourselves!"

"I see."

The anesthesiologist looked back briefly at the temperature monitor. The temperature reading was now 103.5°F (39.7°C).

"Even as we speak," the anesthesiologist warned, "The patient is burning up with fever. We can't wait any longer. If we do nothing now, the patient soon will be dead."

Having said that to the anesthesiology assistant, the anesthesiologist then leaned over the surgical curtain to the nearest neurosurgical fellow, and said:

"Excuse me, but there appears to be a small problem."

The neurosurgical fellow knew that, in neurosurgery, there were no small problems. The neurosurgical fellow replied: "What do you mean?"

"Have you taken a look at the temperature monitor recently?"

The neurosurgical fellow had not looked at the temperature monitor. The neurosurgical fellow looked at the temperature monitor now. The temperature reading was 103.8°F (39.9°C). I was obviously febrile. The neurosurgical fellow was dumbstruck.

"That is correct," the anesthesiologist continued. "That reading is not a typo or a misprint. The patient's temperature is 103.8°F (39.9°C). There can be only one reason why a patient develops a fever so rapidly during surgery. The patient has malignant hyperthermia. If the surgery is not finished...and finished soon...and he is not immersed immediately in ice water to cool him down...our patient will be dead within the hour.

The anesthesiologist paused briefly to let things sink in, before continuing: "In short, I think we have a small problem."

The neurosurgical fellow awoke from his stupor. The neurosurgical fellow grasped the significance of the anesthesiologist's report. The neurosurgical fellow faced the anesthesiologist again, and said:

"I understand. I will let the others know right away."

"That will be fine," the anesthesiologist replied. "Just remember," the anesthesiologist continued...whatever you have to do, do it quickly. Time is not on your side."

"Thanks."

The neurosurgical fellow returned to his side of the surgical curtain.

Words were exchanged amongst various members of the neurosurgical team. Some words were whispered, while others were barked. Although the words and exchanges were largely inaudible outside the surgical curtain, the tone here was definitely unmistakable. The tone was more than a little bit frantic.

The neurosurgical team members moved more quickly to fix the vagrant left middle meningeal artery, and relieve the pressure inside my skull that had threatened to crush its contents. The neurosurgical team members then hurriedly finished the rest of the surgery as quickly as possible, and closed the skull back up. Surgery was finished, and I was quickly immersed in ice.

Of course, I wasn't actually finished with my necessary surgeries just yet. I still had a fracture in my left jaw, a gash over my left eye, and a puffed up nose that concealed a septum that had been deviated during the course of the bicycle accident. Still, I was finished for now. The epidural hematoma that threatened to crush my brains against my skull had been released. There would be no more surgeries for me on that day.

As soon as the neurosurgeons completed their work, I was transferred from the operating table to an ice bath that had been prepared to cool my core body temperature down to normal. The anesthesiologist gave the antidote, Dantrolene, as well, in hopes of calming the body's muscles down a bit more.

I was then taken from the ice bath to the recovery room. There I would learn what function, if any, remained in my mind. There would be no more surgeries for me on that day, though.

As I left the operating room that night, none of my wits were about me. I was in a deep, dark coma. Over the course of the last eight hours at Mid-Island Hospital, I had been injected with Valium and anesthetized with agents here that to this day have not been properly identified to my own satisfaction. That was my condition upon leaving the operating room.

I was now in a medically-induced coma. That was the medical term for my condition. It would take several days for me to clear these drugs from my system enough so that I could at last open my eyes, and provide some semblance of a person among the living. Until that time, everyone would simply have to wait.

Dr. Nicolletti emerged from the surgical theater some time later to speak to my mom.

"Mrs. Moutsiakis," Dr. Nicolletti began.

"Yes," my mom replied.

"The surgery was successful. We were able to identify the source of the bleeding, fix that artery, clean up some of the mess, and then close the skull back up. The surgery was a success. The surgery was complicated by an episode of malignant hyperthermia, however. As we speak, our son is being immersed in an ice-bath to cool him down to normal. We will simply have to wait to see how much function your son can regain. I should warn you. His rehabilitation will be a long one. The only thing to do now is to hope and pray for a miracle."

"That's all I have been doing."

"Well, keep doing what you're doing, and keep praying for that miracle."

CHAPTER ELEVEN

Here I thought the worst at last had past, and
Things were not as bad as they first seemed
Until I tried to open up my mouth
And found my speech impediment
More than a nasty, little dream

Like a hibernating grizzly bear awakening from deep, dark slumber, I pried open my poor, sleepy eyes. Even before coming completely to my senses, I realized that something here was out of whack. I willed myself awake. As I woke up, I spied my first glance at this strange new room I found myself in. Absolutely nothing in this room looked familiar to me. I had never been here before...of this I was certain.

"Where am I?" I thought to myself.

I had absolutely no clue. It would take some time before I truly learned where I had gone.

Life is full of new beginnings. Some are pleasant; others less so. Some we choose to enter into; others are just thrust upon us.

What make us special are not all the circumstances that we find ourselves engaged in. Circumstances are things over which we do not have control. What make us special are the things we choose to do with what we have here…given all the circumstances in which we do find ourselves.

Up to this point in my life, everything had been too easy. I had graduated from high school at the age of sixteen third in a class of four hundred fifty. I was a National Merit Finalist. I had graduated from the university at the age of nineteen magna cum laude. I was an alumnus of the Space Life Sciences Training Program in Cape Canaveral, FL. I started medical school at the age of nineteen. I scored the highest on Step One of the National Board of Medical Examiners licensing exam of anyone at Stony Brook. Up to this point in my life, everything seemed almost effortlessly easy.

All of that was about to change.

Welcome to Hillcrest Head Injury Recovery Association. One chapter in my life had closed. A new chapter would soon begin…one that I had tried too long to just forget. This chapter taught me many things. Perhaps the most important was just how to treasure every day as its unique and special gift. Alas, this day, like every other, too, will pass, and be no more.